By Motorcycle Through Vietnam

by

Lawrence Bransby

Copyright and Acknowledgements

Copyright © Lawrence Bransby 2017
Facebook, Website
Lawrence Bransby has asserted his right to be identified as the Author of this work in accordance with the Copyright, Designs and Patents Act 1988.
All rights reserved. No part of this publication may be reproduced or transmitted in any form or by any means, electronic or mechanical, including photocopy, recording, or any information storage and retrieval system, without permission in writing from the copyright owner.

Cover design by Clive Thompson (cliveleet@gmail.co.za)

ISBN 9781520977225

Please note: I have published this book without photographs to lower the purchase price. As we live in the digital world, I encourage you to go to www.hareti.co.uk, my son's website, where you will be able to see a large selection of photographs taken during the journey described here. The e-book, however, has been published with photographs.

Excerpts from BLOODS: AN ORAL HISTORY OF THE VIETNAM WAR BY BLACK VETRANS by Wallace Terry, copyright © 1984 by Wallace Terry. Used by permission of Random House, an imprint and division of Random House LLC. All rights reserved.

"On and off, for 2000 years, war has raged on its soil as the Chinese, Mongols, the French and the Americans have attempted to bend Vietnam to their will. To a greater or smaller degree, they have all failed and even the might of the United States, with its vastly superior firepower and all the technology of modern warfare, could not defeat a people fired by a passion for freedom, independence and the unification of their ancient land."

A Short History of Vietnam - Gordon Kerr

"From 1959 to 1975, more than 2.7 million Americans served in Vietnam. Over 58,000 died; 300,000 were wounded; 2,436 remain missing in action. It was the first war in US history that was recorded as a defeat. The enemy was a determined one; neither time nor the catastrophic loss of over 600,000 dead - the equivalent of the United States losing ten million - deterred him from fighting on."

Inside the LRRPS Rangers in Vietnam - Michael Lee Lanning

Hang a left across the Pacific...

It was supposed to be a trip around Cuba. Instead I hung a left and ended up in Vietnam.

That's how it should be - no detailed plans and let the journey take its own path.

The trip's genesis was sudden: One night my Significant Other and I were watching the telly. Chris Tarrant was making his affable way across Cuba, riding the dilapidated trains. And as I watched, that unmistakable feeling of wanderlust rose up in me so strongly that I could no longer sit still. I had to get up, walk around, work off some of the nervous tension that was building up inside me.

Inexplicitly, I discovered that I was feeling anger towards Chris Tarrant; I resented him, didn't want to watch any more - which was not particularly fair because Mr Tarrant had done nothing against me personally. And questioning this emotion, I realised it was because I wanted it to be *me*. I wanted it to be me so badly that it was causing my hands to tremble, my chest tight with suppressed frustration.

But, unlike Tarrant, I would be riding a bike, not trains. And I would do it alone; no camera crew following me about or fussy director telling me what to do.

In my mind's eye, I could feel the tropical air warm in my face, my bike vibrating comfortably under me, sugar-cane fields rustling on either side of a dusty, pot-holed road; dilapidated villages and 1950's American cars driven by dark-skinned men cruised by, Afro-Cuban jazz filling the air with lively sound...

I felt trapped behind the gentle walls of domesticity. The bright world of possibility was just within reach but being doled out in teaspoons when I wanted to gulp it down, feel it pouring wet and refreshing across my face and hair.

The next day the frustration was still there. There's got to be a better way, I told myself.

Then, in a moment of clarity, I thought, *How about honesty?*

So I sought out my wife who was staring at her computer screen. "I need to talk to you seriously," I said, sitting down opposite her.

She looked pained. "What have I done now?"

"It's not you - it's me..." I waited until I had her full attention then said, "I'm *unbelievably* frustrated. I'm going out of my *mind* here..."

I told her about the Extreme Railway Journeys and what it had done to me; how badly I needed to throw a leg over my bike again and head towards the distant horizon. I was still developing my carefully listed points when she said, in an off-hand manner, "Well, go then..."

Bless her. So I did.

But Cuba was impractical. Not on a bike. There seem to be no bikes for rent in Cuba and, even if you manage to persuade one of the locals to "rent" you their bike on the sly, the consequences for you and the owner if caught by the police make it not worth the risk. And, according to accounts on the 'Net of people who have tried this, the bikes they do manage to get hold of are usually so worn out that they pack up and die within days of setting out. Not good if you plan a month-long exploration of the entire island.

I took out an atlas. How about hanging a left across the Pacific and exploring Vietnam instead? I thought.

And that's how it happened...

The American/Vietnam War

This travelogue is very different from any of the others I have written.

When I first decided to travel by motorcycle through Vietnam, I wrestled with the ever-present spectre of the Vietnam War (or, as it is known locally, the American war) - as if labelling a war with the name of your enemy makes them the aggressor.

I felt uncomfortable at the prospect of writing about a journey through a beautiful country, filled with gentle and gracious people, without making reference to that part of its history which ripped out its soul - and that of the soldiers from other nations, mainly America, who fought there. Even today the very word "Vietnam" is too often interpreted as referring to the war rather than to the country and its people.

In preparing for the trip I did a lot of reading, focusing especially on the recollections of the ordinary soldiers who fought on both sides. And in my reading I came across three books that contain first-person accounts that at once moved and horrified me. I decided that I needed to include some short extracts from these personal experiences to keep alive in the reader's mind things that happened in Vietnam a mere four to five decades ago.

The contrast, I hope you will find - between the violence then and the peace now, the tenacity, self-sacrifice and resilience of this seemingly gentle people fighting for the right to control their own destiny - will create a more balanced, perhaps nuanced, picture of this fascinating country.

The three books are: *Bloods* by Wallace Terry, *Nam* by Mark Baker and *Everything We Had* by Al Santoli.

I encourage you to get hold of and read these books in their entirety. You will, I have no doubt, be as moved by them as I was.

So, why this constant harking back to the War in what should be a motorcycle travelogue?

I grew up in the 60s. I watched the news footage, looked with horrified fascination at the photographs in the newspapers and in Time and Life and Panorama magazines. As a young adult I watched, with a growing despair, *The Deer Hunter* and *Full Metal Jacket* and *Apocalypse Now*. Instinctively, I didn't want to watch the gung-ho, kill-anything-with-slitty-eyes, Rambo genre - simplistic films that seldom engaged the brain, lacked nuance, were, in essence, little more than propaganda: Americans good, Gooks bad... like so many other war movies, just change the names: Nip, Charlie, Slopehead, Chink, Raghead, Dink, Gook, Hun, Injun and others equally pejorative.

I was profoundly moved, often to tears, by the dehumanising effect of war. Somehow, without having experienced it, I understood something of the moral dilemma of having to decide whether to kill another human being, even though at arm's length.

My father fought in WW2. As a young man he volunteered as soon as he was old enough and spent what was left of the war as an able seaman on British destroyers. When my brother and I were still little, before we went to sleep at night, my father would come into our room to read to us, but often we would plead, "Tell us about the war, Dad -" and he'd sit on the edge of one of our beds and relate to us some of his experiences - the allied landings in Sicily and Salerno, the sights and sounds of battle, the slow *pom... pom... pom* of the two-pounder, anti-aircraft naval machine guns and the faster *pom-pom-pom-pom* of the Oerlikons, suiting the action to the words by beating his hand against his leg.

He was proud of what he did, of his service in the fight for freedom over tyranny. There was no ambivalence there: the enemy were clearly bad; the allies obviously good. Soldiers wore uniforms so you could identify them. There were rules and codes of behaviour - not always adhered to, granted, but they were there.

My wife's father and his brothers were in the British merchant navy, had been since they were boys. For a young Welsh lad from Newport in those days, you signed on as a sailor or you went down the coal mines. All the brothers, in their early teens, signed on. And when war was declared, they found themselves participating in the conflict as part of the merchant navy, the Red Dusters. My wife's uncle Laurie had two ships torpedoed under him and survived. He took part in the Russian convoys too - yet he would never speak of what happened. Nor would his brothers.

Unlike many, I got off lightly. In South Africa, during the Apartheid years, I was required to do my National Service after leaving school. Whilst being ambivalent about Apartheid, I was convinced that our way of life was being threatened in a proxy war orchestrated by Communists who were using Cuban forces in Angola to infiltrate South West Africa, now Namibia, and to radicalise the local black population to rise against the mainly Afrikaans-speaking Nationalist government.

My army training was surreal and benign. After the fairly routine breaking down and building up process of basics, I was awarded a commission (I had deferred for four years to get my teaching degree). Now, with 2nd lieutenant's pips on my shoulders and still struggling to grow a passable moustache, I was posted to Paratus, the Defence Force magazine, as a photojournalist. They didn't know what else to do with me.

The only "action" I experienced was on assignment to the Border - the Caprivi Strip - a narrow slice of land between Angloa and South West Africa that was being defended from small bush-camp bases by young lads in uniform, keeping the terrs from entering our land. I had been issued a pistol and one clip of ammunition before I left. I used it once - to shoot a cow in the head after the Bedford we were travelling in hit it in the dark on a lonely dirt road somewhere in the bush. It was still alive. The young troops looked to me - after all, I was the lieutenant, and a venerable 21 to their teenage 17.

What to do? Leave it there? Put it out of its misery?

In the end I shot it in the head. It took quite a few bullets before it stopped breathing. Like George Orwell and the elephant, I didn't know what I was doing, compelled by the stars on my shoulders to take some meaningful action, and it didn't make me happy.

One night in a bush camp called Ondangua I was woken after midnight with the armoured cars firing up their engines. Floodlights had been switched on, all pointing into the darkness of the thorn trees that surrounded us, cleared for fifty metres or so to give an uninterrupted field of defensive fire but hiding unknown horrors in the dark shadows beyond the reach of the lights. Officers were shouting orders for everyone to stand to in preparation for an attack.

I panicked, struggled to put on my uniform in the dark, grabbed and cocked my pistol expecting at any moment to sense an enemy darken the flap of my tent, a feral presence whose only aim was to kill me. Unable to tie my boot laces, I rushed out - pistol held out in front of me, boot laces flapping around my ankles - to the camp perimeter where soldiers were crouched, staring out into the fearful blackness of the surrounding bush. I was fortunate not to have shot myself in the leg.

It was a drill, we were told a short time later. Well done - reaction time so many minutes. Get back to bed now.

But whispered rumours in late-night bars were always doing the rounds about the terrible things being done by the South African Special Forces - the notorious Koevoet Brigade who, all acknowledged, were killers who didn't abide by any rules so long as they eliminated terrs and Communists and blacks who dared threaten our country.

But I only saw one dead soldier during my time in the army. Relaxing in my tent late one afternoon I heard a gun shot close by. I rushed out. Some Bedfords were parked a few metres away, back from a patrol into the bush. Standing by the open tailgate of the truck closest to me was a young soldier being supported by some of his mates. His khaki shirt was soaked with blood. Because I was nearest, I helped ease him down. We laid him on his back in the sand. There was vomit around his mouth and he wasn't breathing. A soldier began giving him mouth-to-mouth and shouted to me to stop the bleeding from his back. I rolled him over slightly so I could get my hand under and it was only then that I was able to feel the fist-sized hole where his spine should have been.

He was dead. Moments later some soldiers carried a young man past us, a boy just out of school, supporting him under his arms, his legs limp and dragging through the soft sand. Saliva ran in long strings from his mouth and he was making terrible moaning sounds that we could hear for hours before they took him away.

It was an accident. He had forgotten to clear the 7.62 round from the breech, pointed the rifle at his friend's chest and pulled the trigger for fun. It killed him instantly.

That was my only experience of war.

It was like a game. Yes, people were being killed in South West Africa, blown up by land mines laid in the dirt roads and tracks at night; isolated farmers were being murdered. In return, the police and the army were trying to stem the trickle of SWAPO - South West Africa People's Organisation - soldiers attempting to infiltrate our borders. At the same time a more intense war was being fought deep inside Angola despite the government insisting we weren't there, and soldiers were patrolling the townships in South Africa where black unrest against Apartheid was increasing in intensity. (Although, at that time, this mainly manifested itself by brutal necklacing of other blacks accused of being collaborators.)

Why am I telling you this? What has this to do with a motorcycle trip around Vietnam?

I will attempt to explain.

After I decided to do this trip, I began to read up on the country. And most of what I read described the beautiful places for tourists to visit.

Somehow, it seemed plastic, unreal, contrived. It was as if the war had been airbrushed out.

Perhaps because of when I was born, the years of Vietnam War exposure, the horrors of My Lai, the slow ooze of information that began to leak out from the edges of the conflict telling the world that all was not as it seemed. It left its mark on me. Even now, I cannot think of the name "Vietnam" without seeing images of Thich Quang Duc, the Buddhist monk who self-immolated in the streets of Saigon; of Kim Phuc, the little naked girl with her Napalmed skin sloughing off as she ran screaming towards American soldiers who stood, helpless, witnessing close-up the personal face of their atrocities; of young American soldiers cradling the bleeding bodies of their ripped-up friends, waiting for the helicopter that would medivac them out.

Perhaps with the passing of time, younger generations can reflect on this war with a dispassionate interest, something read about in the musty pages of a book.

I can't do that. It's too real, too visceral, even though I was only aware of it from the glossy pages of Life Magazine and the disjointed images from newsreel cameras.

Because of this, I cannot travel around Vietnam without the spectre of the war peering over my shoulder all the time.

It was during this war that America lost her virginity as a nation - if she had ever been chaste before this. Some *thirteen million tons* of bombs were dropped onto the forests and villages and towns and people of Vietnam during that decade; that's about 265kgs for every man, woman and child in Indochina, give or take a few kgs of TNT, if my maths is correct. And when that didn't work there was always Napalm and Agent Orange.

This war has become the textbook example of mission creep, of engaging in a conflict that you can't get out of even though you want to. The initial principal seemed such a good one: support the French colonialists who were drawing a line in the sand against the threat of Communism, the fear of the domino effect if Vietnam were to fall. And we all know that Communism is bad, right?

But then the French left.

And then American advisors started going on missions with their South Vietnamese allies - in an advisory capacity, of course. But then some of the advisors got caught in the crossfire and died so the advisors started shooting back and then they weren't advisors any more.

Then the North Vietnamese supposedly attacked two American ships in the Gulf of Tonkin with motor torpedo boats (although it is highly doubtful that this ever happened), which allowed President Johnson "legally" to begin bombing North Vietnam.

Without any formal declaration, the war had begun.

It's always easy to bomb the people of a third-world country because they can't hit you back. They don't have the technology. But to bomb effectively you need an airfield and once you've got an airfield you need to defend it and to defend it you need ground troops and when your ground troops keep getting killed because, unlike the B52s dropping bombs from 30,000 ft, troops on the ground bleed and can be shot so you need more troops to defend the troops that are bleeding because the enemy - North Vietnamese, Communists, Viet Cong, Viet Minh, they all looked the same - somehow didn't want to play by the rules. They didn't wear uniforms; they didn't stand and fight like a gentleman should. They didn't fly flags and have trucks and tanks with convenient emblems painted on them so you knew just whom you're fighting and whom you're trying to kill. They look exactly like the peasant villagers who gently till their fields and care for their wives and children and their water buffalo and their rice paddies and then, when you aren't looking they shoot you in the back and blow you up with land mines cunningly concealed and then disappear back onto the land with their wives and their children and their water buffalo and, after seeing so many of your mates being slaughtered by people you just can't see, you get frustrated and want to lash out, to hit back at *anything* no matter what, just so you can tell yourself that you're doing something, you're fighting back, you're avenging the deaths of your butchered mates. And because you don't know which of the peasant farmers are the bad guys and because they don't fight fair and wear uniforms the easiest way is just to kill them all and because you know the women are helping by hiding weapons and some of your mates have been killed by little kids running up to you with a smile and a hand grenade behind their backs or hiding a satchel bomb in a shoe-shine box and it's difficult to bomb or machine gun a village and selectively kill only the bad guys, it's probably just easier to waste them all and call it collateral damage and if the kids get in the way then that's just too sad but there would be no adults to look after them anyway and if you machine gun them from a long way off or drop bombs on them from very high you never get to see the skin sloughing off their small naked bodies or hear their thin screams. And for some strange reason they just won't stop fighting no matter how many of their villages you burn, or how many of them you kill; unlike civilized people who know that there's a time to say "enough" they just keep on coming and keep on dying and keep on coming some more so you bring in more soldiers to kill more of them and because they hide in the forest and jump out and kill you then disappear into the forest again before you can shoot them back the best plan would be to wipe out the forest - *all* of it, kill it all so there will be no forest for them to hide in but then they go and hide underground in small dark tunnels cunningly camouflaged and creep out in the dark and kill you before disappearing under the ground again so you bring in even more troops who keep on dying and you just want to nuke them all and let God sort it out - or so the bumper stickers had it - and the terrible thing is that for the first time there are brave men with cameras filming all the dead and dying young men and showing their footage back home so now the mums and dads know that their young men are not the noble, victorious, unkillable soldiers they had always thought they were, sweeping the little yellow men before them with inexorable bravery; instead, they are tired and drugged to their eyeballs because they don't want to face the reality of what they're doing any more; they are mud-covered and bleeding and have limbs blown off and their eyes tell the story even more evocatively than their spilled blood does that they are losing this war and they just want to get out and go home except for those who had begun to enjoy the killing...

And the people at home, who began to read behind the lies of their leaders who still claimed that they were winning this war, started to protest, especially the young, and then the National Guard took it upon themselves to shoot some of the young Kent State University students who were protesting against the war and, as everyone knows, when your peace-keepers begin shooting unarmed citizens who want to do nothing more than voice their opinions as is entrenched in the constitution of any self-respecting democracy then you know the government will fall.

And it did.

Johnson backed out, breathing a sigh of relief that he didn't have to lie any more to his people and left it to Nixon to broker a tattered peace.

And as I type this, the British commons has just passed a resolution granting permission for bombing missions to begin against ISIS/ISIL/Diash in Syria.

Deja vu?

Again, we are faced with an enemy that doesn't play by the rules. After Vietnam, few Western societies will risk boots on the ground. I suppose that's a good thing: we really don't like seeing our young men and women in body bags or with the stumps of their blasted limbs oozing blood into the dust of a foreign land. So, just like in Vietnam, we're going to bomb the shit out of them from the air. Yet everyone knows that you can't bomb your way to victory in a war and everyone knows that, no matter how sophisticated today's smart bombs are, more civilians - women and children and old men and little babies - are going to die than bad guys.

The bombing is a gesture. It eases the conscience. We all know that.

And like the Viet Cong, radicalised Islamists don't mind how many of their members die so long as the Islamic Caliphate becomes a reality, so long as Islam one day rules this world. Worse, in fact, because to the radical Islamic fighter, dying is a good thing blessed with eternal rewards.

You can't defeat people like that by bombing them.

I'm not judging. I'm just sad.

War is like that...

In the end, no one really wins. I'm just glad I don't have to make the decisions.

ISIL are not nice people. Someone needs to send them a message that it's just not cricket to go into other people's cities and indiscriminately blow up their citizens, run them down with trucks, cut off their heads if they don't do what you say, believe what you believe. But they, too, just like the Viet Cong, have a disturbing habit of blending in with the local population and attacking when you least expect it. And, strangely - we don't really understand it, something about many virgins and streams of water running beneath - they are happy to kill themselves so long as they kill some of us in return. This makes them damned hard to fight without losing a lot of soldiers. And we, unlike them, don't really like losing soldiers. So, what to do?

Drop bombs from high up and to hell with the consequences - even if we've got to bomb them alongside the Russians who are also bombing the people we are supporting. The enemy of my enemy is my friend so that makes the Russians sometimes our friends and sometimes not.

I pray that this war against ISIL doesn't become our Vietnam. Fortunately, as I write this, Russia and China seem to be on our side. During the Vietnam War, both Russia and China were supporting the North Vietnamese. The beginning of the era of proxy wars: West against East; Communism against Capitalism, hegemony and an inordinate fear of falling dominoes.

And that's why I can't just ride my bike across Vietnam without being aware of the horrors that took place here just under half a century ago. Just like I can't travel through South Africa without the insistent touch on my shoulder causing me to turn and look again, deeper, and know that it was here that Apartheid was spawned and grew and became part of me, of my childhood and my teenage years, formed me and moulded me in its image until I was old enough to see and understand a little more.

Was South Africa a better place during Apartheid than under the ANC and Zuma? For whom? Does equality before the law, dignity, the right to vote for black people balance the murders and the rapes, the corruption, nepotism, crumbling infrastructure that characterises my old home today?

Apartheid was morally indefensible - but Africa ruled by indigenous Africans doesn't inspire me with much confidence either.

Was it right to make a stand in Vietnam to stop the dominoes tumbling? In some ways, yes. But the waters became muddied. Human lives were brutalised. They always are when the great powers play out their war games in the back yards of others less powerful than themselves.

And that's the tragedy of it all.

"You smoke marijuana?"

I wrestle with an importunate taxi tout outside Noi Bai Airport, Hanoi, who attempts to take hold of my bag, but I resist. Eventually I get through to him that I don't want to do the tourist thing, prefer to travel local, and he leaves me standing on the pavement amongst the shove and push of bodies one always finds at the entrance to an airport. The air is hot and wet and my clothes stick to my skin. Jet-lag fugs my brain. The No. 7 bus, I am told, will take me into central Hanoi but I decide to compromise and make my way towards the open door of a mini-bus taxi, its boy-faced driver in the process of striking a deal with a twenty-something lass carrying a large rucksack. She looks tired and travel-worn. Her hair needs a wash; her skin is tanned and she slings the rucksack off her back with practiced ease.

I introduce myself. Her name is Anna and she's from the Czech Republic. Just flown in from Cambodia and, like me, looking for a cheap hotel in the city centre.

We take our seats in the back. The taxi, unlike its driver, is old; its seats are torn, its bodywork tired. The radio plays loudly.

We wait.

Our driver strides about, approaching prospective clients, his smile and waving arm drawing them towards his waiting vehicle. All walk by, ignoring him. He has quoted Anna $5 for the trip but I had been told in the airport that the fare ought to be $3. Where notoriously mendacious taxi drivers in foreign countries are concerned, I always make sure I have foreknowledge of local rates. I jerk a thumb and say, "They told me it was $3."

It suddenly becomes $3 for both of us. Like all good taxi drivers, he's inflated the price.

It is clear that we aren't going to move until the mini-bus is full. Sixteen-seater. Thirteen to go. Or, if Vietnam is anything like Africa, twenty-seven. It isn't looking good.

The driver suggests that I assist him in touting for passengers to speed up the process and, as it serves my interest as well as his, I approach a pair of back-packers and offer to share the taxi.

They are not looking happy; they've just lost their luggage and the young girl is crying. I commiserate and approach another group of back-packers. They seem interested and saunter over. They are not convinced. The $3 fare becomes a desperate $2. They too walk away.

A sign on the dashboard (next to a fake jade Buddha and a plastic Chinese Foo Dog) informs me that I will be liable for all charges relating to parking, bridge and road tolls and anything else the driver can screw out of me. The No 7 bus is beginning to look attractive.
Briefly I reflect on the need of the young man to appeal to the protective powers of both the guardian lion and the Buddha to keep him (and us) safe on the road.

Nothing happens.

I suggest to Anna that we might as well take the bus. She agrees and we get out. With cries from our driver of, "Just ten minutes - wait!" we retrieve our bags from the back and lug them to the bus rank. Ten minutes later, it arrives.

The No. 7 is Spartan and utilitarian, the seats little more than planks of wood covered with vinyl, the windows smeared and almost opaque with dirt. A young girl politely gives up her seat for me.

I wish she hadn't. It makes me feel old.

We clatter into the suburbs of Hanoi, stopping every few minutes to exchange passengers who take their lives in their hands because the thick shoal of scooters through which we nudge our way simply part like fish on both sides of the bus.

The land passing by outside the smeared windows is flat and dirty, the air thick with moisture and dust and diesel fumes. Many Vietnamese, especially the young, wear facemasks that cover mouth, nose and chin, giving them the appearance of youthful Hannibal Lectors looking for victims. I am informed by someone that the wearing of face masks, as well as performing the obvious function of filtering particulates, communicates some message about availability for marriage but this was never confirmed. Wishful thinking, perhaps.

The bus journey seems endless. Buildings lean against one another, competing for space. Snagged pavements push pedestrians into the road; alleys between tall buildings become narrow, mysterious, ever-dark slits in the stained concrete. Traffic thickens and clogs, horns blow constantly, strident and demanding. Inside our claustrophobic, metal box I breathe used air, my skin sticky with dust and sweat.

At some point as we nose our way through this bewildering clutter of life, two travel-worn young lasses get on, dump their heavy rucksacks on the floor and look with bewilderment at the conductor who stands in front of them clutching a fistful of notes, expecting money. One opens her wallet and proffers a note. The conductor shakes his head. The sweaty child/woman offers another, seemingly at random - 10,000... 100,000... 1,000,000... her face taking on that frozen look that says, *I'm completely out of my depth here. I'm offering notes with zillions of zeroes on them and I haven't the foggiest idea of what they're worth.*

In the end the conductor, still holding in his fist a thick wad of notes, separated into denominations by his fingers, reaches out and selects one from the handful she is clutching, carefully removing it with two fingers. He slots it into the wad in his hand, peels off two smaller notes - even these have lines of zeroes marching across the top enough to make your eyes water - and hands them to the girl who accepts them blankly.

"Monopoly money," I comment and she gives me a wan smile.

Anna strikes up a conversation with a young Vietnamese man who tells her where we should get off. The bus stops and we stumble onto the street with our luggage, our senses assaulted by the unaccustomed noise and movement that swirls about us. We have been told that we now need to take the No. 4 bus to the Old Quarter. I hope he's right. I feel overwhelmed, but happy, for the time being, to attach myself to Anna, this young lass who seems strangely in control. Perhaps I am getting old.

Eventually, belching diesel fumes, a bus with a barely readable "4" in its destination window arrives. We spend another hour on plank seats while our bus shoulders its way through increasingly thick traffic. I begin to wonder whether we've missed our stop and are heading back round again, expect to see the "Noi Bai Airport" sign once again through the smeared window. Surely no normal city can be this clogged for this long.

Eventually the conductor, whom Anna has befriended, indicates where we should alight and we step once again into a maelstrom of traffic. We stand on the bank of a moving river of scooters and the occasional car, all toot-tooting as they weave and diverge around obstacles, eddy in street back-waters, surge and hesitate, come together and separate like those accumulations of fish that seem to act with a collective consciousness. Personal motorcycle space is compressed to millimetres. It seems to be impossible for anyone to fall over - they would just lean on each other and stay upright.

Now, how to cross the street? There are two zebra crossings. I watch as the traffic flies by and realise that these black and white stripes are little more than street decoration, somewhat faded, without any functional benefit to the pedestrian whatsoever. Now, having read about negotiating this unrelenting stream of humanity and madness, I turn to Anna and say, "Just walk -" and that's what we do. I step into the traffic with Anna close behind and, strangely, miraculously, it absorbs us into itself, eddies around, splits and reforms; so long as we keep moving, steady and purposeful, it opens to allow us in, closes behind us, permits us to pass.

With experience, I came to realise that there are two ways most people cross a busy road in Vietnam: the first - usually old people who seem resigned to whatever fate or karma has to offer - simply set off slowly as if there are no vehicles at all on the street. No one gets angry or hoots, waves fists. Cars, trucks, scooters just absorb them and allow them through. Younger, more alert people look for a brief opening, a slight thinning in the flood; they make eye contact with the driver of the vehicle that is most likely to run them down to signal their intention, step into the road with a purposeful air while fluttering one hand up and down in a *I'm coming, please don't run me down...* gesture.

Both work well. The only time I came close to being killed was when I forgot the "slow and purposeful" rule and darted into the street to retrieve a plastic bag of shopping dropped by a woman on a scooter. The middle-aged woman who nearly ran over me was not impressed and told me so in a stream of angry Vietnamese invective.

Anna and I make our way along the street towards a hostel she has found using her phone, continuing to brave the traffic that seems to come at us from all directions. Of course, we have to walk in the road because, as we had noticed from the bus, all pavements have been colonised, usually for the parking of scooters, millions of them. Everywhere you look there are scooters: parked, being ridden, being stripped and worked on in a hundred pavement workshops. In the occasional gaps where scooters are not parked, men, women, children, old people, laughing teenagers, men playing cards and smoking crouch or sit on brightly-coloured, children's plastic chairs eating their evening meal from small bowls, the food dispensed from steaming pots of "street food" kept warm over smoky charcoal fires. Somehow, family life seems to have emerged from the houses and onto the pavement. Children play in the gutters, the wheels of passing vehicles just inches away, and no one calls after them to be careful.

Occasionally, almost like a caricature, a small woman with stick bones and wearing a conical hat woven from straw will walk through this heaving throng carrying heavily-laden baskets of vegetables or fruit or cooked food suspended by rope from the ends of a long bamboo pole balanced on one shoulder.

At last, we find the hostel and pay our $6 for a bed ($5 for the upper bunk). Outside the dorm, shoes are neatly stacked on racks, and books in a variety of languages lie about to be picked up by the next traveller, read and then left somewhere along the back-packers' trail until they fall apart or are re-cycled as toilet paper or roll-ups. In the communal lounge, a young Malaysian woman is in conversation with a Chinese girl and two twenty-something lads from Australia and America. They all speak English.

We unpack and lock our belongings away in our personal lockers and walk out into the mind-numbing bustle of the city to look for food and a beer. In a quiet back street we find a small restaurant and eat Vietnamese food. The frenetic pace of life goes on in the street outside, oblivious.

On my way back to the hostel, a man on a scooter rides alongside me. "You smoke marijuana?" he calls and I shake my head.

Later I walk out into the madness of the night. Another man pulls alongside me on his scooter. "You want anything, my frien'?" he asks.

Again, I shake my head.

"Nice woman -?"

I tell him not tonight, thank you and he rides away.

In a small cafe, I order coffee from a middle-aged couple who watch TV on a large screen, bare feet resting on the chairs. They eat sunflower seeds, dropping the husks onto the floor. On the screen, a badly acted soap. Sadly, throughout Vietnam, seemingly in every house, restaurant and cafe, a large-screen TV plays day-time soaps and re-runs of Jackie Chan karate films, the volume turned up high. It's a national obsession.

I experience my first taste of Vietnamese coffee - strong and sweet and served with a small glass tumbler sitting in a bowl of hot water. The man tells me it is twenty-five and I assume I need to add on a confetti of zeroes. My mind is closing down - is it 250, 2,500 or 25,000? I try to do a quick mental calculation: $1 = 23,000D (or is it 2,300?)

I scratch through my wallet, feeling like the young lass must have felt on the bus as she randomly offered meaningless notes decorated with national deficits of zeroes. The man points to two D10,000 and one D5,000 note which I give him. Aah! - D25,000 - about a dollar...

Back into the street. It's more "into" than "onto" - here one doesn't walk *on* a street or pavement, one is absorbed *into* it. Scooters with whole families mounted, father, mother and all the children; scooters used as donkeys are in poorer parts of the world, laden 'til they drop; scooters mounted by teenage tearabouts, prim business women, old men, girls in jeans and pink spangled t-shirts; scooters ridden with the left thumb hovering over the horn button, helmets not obligatory. Those helmets that are worn are like stiffened baseball caps, the sort of thing Barbie and Ken would don for a day out to the seaside.

Pots of noodles steam on the pavement, ducks' legs protruding, yellow and stiff like wax, the large aluminium pots heated by crude metal containers of charcoal, started each morning with the aid of an electric fan. Women wearing plastic slops crouch on the pavement selling sticks of sugar cane and kebabs.

As the evening wanes into night, dishes are washed in plastic buckets on the pavement while old women wearing face masks sweep litter off the streets into neat piles in the gutters using brooms made from the stiff fronds of palm trees.

Got to negotiate these streets on a bike tomorrow...

* * * * *

The FBI was on a rampage looking for me. Around the Fourth of July 1969. So I called the FBI, and told them I was out on the Long Island Expressway. And they came and picked me up and put me in manacles again. Then they took me to Whitehall Street, where everybody in New York City gets inducted.

One of the agents said, "Holcomb, this time we're gonna make sure you take the oath so in case this time you leave, you'll be a problem for the army and not for us. We don't wanna be bothered with you any more."

They took me inside to say the oath, and I refused. So they took me outside.

The other agent said, "Listen, Bob, if you don't say the oath, we're gonna lock you up forever. You just won't be seen around anymore."

So I said, "All right." And we went back inside.

I raised my hands and said the oath.

I was sworn into the army in manacles.

From "Bloods" by Wallace Terry

If you kill a dog, don't cry

A short taxi ride. I find myself gripping the seat with both hands as my driver shoulders scooters aside with the bulk of his car and the insistent blare of its horn. I am convinced that paint is shaved off the fenders in miniscule slices as we nudge our way through impossible gaps.

Somehow, we manage not to kill anyone.

I pick up my bike, wire in my GPS and collect spare tubes and spanners for the front and back spindle nuts. There is nothing worse than being stranded somewhere far from help with a flat tyre. (Well, I suppose being run over by a truck is worse but you can't carry spares for that.)

I strap on my luggage and set off gingerly, feeling my way for the first time into the notorious flow of Vietnamese traffic. The small 125cc engine is underpowered but it's not speed I want - it's to stay alive.

I recall some advice I saw on the Internet about driving in Vietnam:

PRACTICAL ROAD USERS' ADVICE FOR VISITORS TO VIETNAM

Vietnam has the second highest rate of traffic fatalities in the world and it's the second most dangerous place on earth for motorcycles, just after India. There are approximately 40 traffic fatalities a day.

On the road there are no rules, so make sure you ignore any traffic rules you know. This should help to achieve a fine balance between two-wheeled fun, beautiful landscapes and complete and utter chaos.

Remember that larger vehicles have the right of way.

Traffic is like a river - flow with it. Riders will find a way to move forward.

If you kill a dog or a chicken, don't stop, cry or feel sorry. It's not your fault. Slow down when you spot these animals and don't hit water buffalo, cows, pigs or horses - simply they are too big.

If the police stop you, just keep talking in any language you know (but not Vietnamese or English) or whatever you want and they'll soon let you go in less than five minutes.

Now that makes me feel better.

Senses switched to hyper-alert, I make my timid way along traffic-snarled roads. But, strangely, after about ten minutes, it all seems quite normal. There is a perverted logic about it that seems to work. Well, most of the time. It's based on two fundamental premises:

1) There are no rules

2) No one really wants to die in an accident.

So people riding scooters make way. (This, it must be said, doesn't apply to the drivers of cars and trucks, but more of that later.)

I come to my first traffic circle. Of course, I'm riding on the right, which always confuses my brain for a while until the change becomes absorbed and accommodated. There are no traffic lights, no yield signs. Vehicles seem to be coming from everywhere all at once. I have to keep moving so, following the instructions, I nose my way in steadily, attempting to exude a feeling of *sang froid* - and it works. Like interlacing fingers I slot in, negotiate my semi-circle, steadily ease right and am released. The logic of no logic seems to work.

After an hour or two I am free of the claustrophobia of Hanoi and begin to see my first rice paddies, muddy, dirty things that bear no relation to the glossy photographs one sees in travel brochures. On the side of the road I come across what looks like an establishment that might sell food. The road has been built high on a levee so I leave the bike, climb over the barrier and make my way across a narrow elevated walkway that leads to an open veranda, gapped wooden planks for a floor, the rest of the house below.

A small man with a wispy clump of hair on his chin - the rest of his olive-brown face is smooth and hairless - greets me in a way that suggests I have conferred upon him an honour far greater than my random selection of his roadside eating-house might warrant. He ushers me into a large, open-sided room, bare except for some low tables set upon reed mats, the poles of the roof supporting a rough palm-leaf thatch.

At some stage in this narrative I am going to have to stop describing every Vietnamese person I meet as "small"; they are *all* small, fine-boned, olive-skinned. (The Vietnamese as a people have yet to succumb to the dreaded scourge of Western obesity.) My Western eyes generalise their appearance and slot each person I meet into the: "Small, olive-skinned, almond-shaped eyes, black hair, brown eyes" pigeonhole.

But this generalisation works both ways: during the War, the four characteristics that defined the American soldier in the eyes of the Vietnamese were their size, first, then their pale skin (the black soldiers were regarded as a curiosity and many

Vietnamese wondered why back soldiers weren't fighting for the other side), round eyes and long noses. This being so, one can understand the propaganda value of a photograph widely circulated during the war that showed a downed American airman, a giant of a man, looking suitably chastened and unthreatening, captured by a young girl, who looks barely fourteen, levelling an AK47 at his stomach. And the message was clear: regardless of how large the American soldiers are, no matter how sophisticated their weapons, they can be defeated, even by this little girl, so long as you keep the faith and never give up.

So I am welcomed by this middle-aged man who has no English at all; I remove my shoes, sit down on a child's plastic chair and ask for coffee. Even this, the universal phrase after Hello, how are you? Coca-Cola and Manchester United, elicits no response. There are the makings of tea on another table so I point and nod.

One of the frustrations of travelling alone and without plans in more remote parts of a country - and where English is only spoken in those areas most attractive to tourists - is that communication becomes increasingly difficult. But, looked at in another way, although one's conversation will lack subtlety, making one's needs known through gesture and facial expression produces a greater intimacy with one's interlocutor. There is a paring down of meaning to the absolute basics, a more precise focus on the face and gestures, the body language, of the person with whom one is interacting. In a way, this heightens the level of intimacy, draws one in behind the words.

In a darkened corner of the room, the man's daughter prepares my tea. She is tiny, her hair tied back in a topknot. I take out my pen and notebook and begin to jot down my impressions. He sits himself next to me, gently removes the pen from my hand and writes down his name and telephone number, as if that will confer upon him in my mind a sense of identity or value. I give him a card with my name on and he is happy.

A short while later a friend of the owner walks across the narrow, wooden bridge from the road. He too is small - but then I am trying not to keep on repeating this. He has a thin moustache and wears a baseball cap. To me he is garrulous, even though he knows I understand nothing of what he says.

The daughter brings me a teapot of smoky, bitter green tea and a small bowl. Each time I drain it, the man leans over and fills it again.

On the ground floor of the house I can hear chickens cackling. Further away are the neat, bright-green patches of rice paddies.

I ask about food, gesturing. He, I assume, tells me what he has to offer. I don't understand so, on a clean page, I draw the picture of a duck. He stands and gestures for me to follow. We walk down a wooden stairway. He opens a chest freezer. Inside are chicken livers and other meat; on a shelf, eggs and greens. I point to some meat and nod. I don't know what it is, but have assured myself that it is not intestines. We return to the table and he offers me a cigarette. I shake my head, point to my lungs and pull a face. He laughs. He takes a hollow bamboo tube about a metre long with a fluted opening for a small pinch of tobacco, primes the pipe then lights it, sucking hard, his mouth covering the opening. I can hear bubbles and wonder whether he's inhaling something more hallucinatory than tobacco. His face is wreathed in blue smoke.

I get up and look over the edge of the veranda. In a roughly ploughed field, red-feathered fowls congregate; further away a woman wearing a conical hat guides a single plough through a sodden rice paddy, pulled behind a water buffalo.

A short while later the daughter brings me rice, an omelette, fried pork and greens. Next to my tea bowl she places a set of wooden chopsticks.

It's enough to feed three people...

It is evening and I book into a modest hotel in Bac Ninh. On entering the town I attempt to use my GPS to find accommodation but it misunderstands and suggests I might like to try a nice hotel in Hanoi.

I find one myself.

This delta land I have travelled through is uniformly flat, the road raised high on levees above the flood plain; below and spreading out on either side, even between the rubble and urban sprawl of Hanoi, are the neat, rectangular fields of rice, some already flooded and in the process of being planted by stooped peasants wearing conical hats, the universal image of Vietnam, as if enacted especially for my benefit. Except here the view is tainted, ugly and clotted with discarded plastic fluttering in the wind, piles of rubble, large ponds dug into the raw earth in which thousands of white ducks congregate, their eventual end the steaming sidewalk pots of the cities, their yellow waxy legs gyrating slowly as the water boils. It is as if the towns and cities have grown too fast for the farmers to adapt and they keep doing what they have done for centuries, stooping, calf-deep in water and mud to thrust another and yet another green rice seedling beneath the still water surface, anchoring its roots in mud, as the concrete sprawl insinuates dirty fingers of that spurious thing we call progress into its once pure and unspoilt form. Many of the ponds and canals have been overcome with the virulent Kariba weed, knotting and multiplying until nothing else will grow or have space to survive.

I long to escape the noisy fug of life here in the lowlands and climb into the more remote mountains close to the border of China. Here, a day's ride from Hanoi, I still come across people wearing facemasks to protect their lungs from the heavily polluted air.

Bac Ninh at night. A cold beer calls. I ride like the locals, without the smothering barrier of helmet and gloves, and experience a sense of freedom and release. Even after just one day I am accommodating to the rules - or non-rules - of motorcycle riding in Vietnam. No quick, sudden movements; ride with gentle assertiveness. Anything goes. Plastic tape marking off road works? If you're on a bike, just lift it and make your way through. Miss an exit ramp on a motorway? Just turn and retrace your route using the hard shoulder. Toll booths? There's a special lane, just narrow enough for a bike, which allows you through. No fee.

I see a young woman on a scooter negotiating traffic whilst cradling an infant against her breast, controlling the bike with one hand; a middle-aged woman rides, talking into her mobile phone, a toddler standing in the foot-well, holding onto the handlebars with both hands. Riding in shorts and flip-flops is the norm.

The city centre is knotted with life, seething and undulating with sound and smell and movement. The pavement doubles as a shop front, a communal fore-court, where flowers and fruit and clothing and trinkets and brightly-coloured plastic goods are displayed; where food bubbles and meat is severed and served and people sit on children's plastic chairs and ladle pasta and green vegetables from soupy bowls into their open mouths with chop-sticks, nipping off the trailing noodles and talking loudly and wet-lipped in monosyllabic nasal imperatives.

I become aware that there are women about - men and women interacting together, eating, commuting, running businesses, talking. How different from so many Muslim countries through which I have travelled where, when the sun sets, the women disappear and the streets become the preserve of men.

I park the bike and walk about, entering lanes between buildings so narrow my hands can touch both walls if I spread them; above my head crazy tangles of wires like the cartoon hair of someone with a finger poked into a live socket, more undisciplined even than the traffic. (So iconic are these - the crazy tangle of wires above and the seething mass of scooters below that pictures of them are printed on t-shirts and sold to tourists in Hanoi and Saigon.)

On either side of the dark, narrow alleys, brief glimpses of everyday life: a man fixes a bicycle wheel; a family sits cross-legged on a carpet, eating with chopsticks from a communal bowl. Little children greet me as I pass, happy and innocent, playing in the streets and alleys, faces unclouded by the threats with which we in the West seem to burden our children. In fact, I feel remarkably unthreatened even in the narrowest and darkest of alleys by these gentle people who absorb me into the hurly-burly of their lives with tolerant smiles.

Here, away from the tourists of Hanoi, I am able to sit quietly on my bright plastic chair, beer in hand (in a glass filled to the brim with ice) and observe the stream of life that passes by in front of me without the constant harassment of touts eager to snag my attention and interest me in their wares.

And it's not long before I meet the delightful Trang and her boyfriend Soyang who invite me to their table. Trang is twenty-five and beautiful; she wears short shorts and a top that exposes the knobs of her perfect shoulders. She wants to practice her English. Her boyfriend is silent but seemingly happy that I join them. On the table is a gas cooker where a pot of exotic things bubbles and steams. She asks if I would like to eat and I nod. I'll try anything once.

She picks up a plate of raw baby octopus, fish and calamari rings and, using her chopsticks, deftly scissors a selection into the steaming pot. On the table are a variety of greens and chilli dips and after a few minutes she chopsticks some octopi into a bowl and offers them to me. I manage to lift one without embarrassing myself, the chop-sticks feeling like numb, broken fingers that won't respond to my will, and gnaw off a tentacle which has the consistency of a piece of old car tyre. Soyang lifts a bottle of vodka from a basin of ice and offers me some by raising his eyebrows. Who am I to refuse? Like the Russians, he wants me to quaff it so one-two-three we drink it down and I feel light-headed, especially with Trang sitting at my side, clinking my beer glass after every sip and telling me I'm a handsome man. She takes a cuddled selfie and I ask her to take one with my phone so I can send it to my wife just to let her know what a rough time I'm having of it. This travelling lark is hard work. I'd hate her to think it was a holiday.

After the second vodka I decide it's probably best I head back to my hotel. Trang looks sad. I think she was enjoying practicing her English.

She and Soyang insist on paying for my beer.

* * * * *

We were coming in and all I could see was jungle. Everywhere was fucking jungle. And I thought, Fuck, I'm in Vietnam! I'd never seen jungle before.

We landed and started to get off the plane. And there's something I'll always remember - the heat and the smell. Napalm. The smell of Napalm and bodies burning. I'll never forget that. Not ever. The smell...

Red flags, dust and the joys of Communism

I am awakened by the strangled shriek of a bantam cock outside my window. Behind the curtain the whole world is dimmed by pollution; the very air has turned a sulphurous yellow. I think of the number of people who die each year in the UK from inhaling particulates and wonder how many years breathing this industrial fug is going to take off my life. No wonder so many people here go about with mask-covered faces.

The road out of Bac Ninh is tangled with vehicles, mainly trucks. I make slow progress, heading northeast towards the mountains, Lang Son and Dong Dang, the border with China just a few kilometres further east.

After two hours, the road narrows to a single lane as I make my way along the Red River flood plain, the air still milky with pollution, the flooded rice paddies alongside the road somehow lacking that quaint perfection one has come to expect from the tourist brochures. Everything is dirty and dusty and littered and I long for countryside devoid of people. Trucks still dominate the road and, at times, it's safer to ride on the hard shoulder, undertaking slower vehicles with only a certain degree of risk - like meeting a parked truck or a motorcycle coming the other way on the wrong side of the road or a bus disgorging passengers. Any way you look at it, it's dangerous riding on these roads. To survive, one must be constantly on the defensive, looking out for errant riders and drivers who can and will do anything, anywhere at any time.

I brake violently to miss t-boning a man on a scooter who rides across both lanes with the *sang froid* of one confident in his karma, convinced that the streams of traffic will, like the waters of the Red Sea, part to let him through. I, not expecting motorcyclists nonchalantly to cross my path at right angles as I ride along a main road, very nearly hit him. Perhaps it's a belief in the regenerative process of reincarnation that allows them to ride in this way with such lack of concern for their own - or others' - lives.

At last the flat, rice-paddy land gives way to trees and I make my way through sweet-smelling plantations from which sheets of wood-veneer have been cut and stacked to dry in fields along the roadside; later this gives way to the surreal landscape of karst mountains, their conical peaks and near vertical sides reminiscent of an alien world.

I am eating very little at the moment and already my jeans are slipping over my hips when I get off the bike. The idea of noodles for breakfast is not appealing, I'm afraid, and the difficulty of trying to communicate over unintelligible menu choices - when there is a menu - makes it easier just not to eat. However, at the small village of Chi Lang I pull over at a roadside eatery, easily identified by the small plastic chairs and tables under a rudimentary corrugated iron roof. A young man sitting at an adjoining table brings me a bowl of tea. I gesture that I would like something to eat and wonder how I will choose, but moments later the lady proprietor places a bowl of noodles and meat on my table followed by a bowl of lettuce. It seems I have no choice. It's noodles or noodles, which makes life easier.

At last the road begins to deteriorate which I take as a good sign. I enter a sparsely populated land of hills, wide, slow-flowing rivers and open forest. The road is lined with banana trees and bamboo, their leaves a deep green against the background of forest. The small towns I pass through - Na Lenh, Na Sam, Na Liet, Na Cam - are cluttered with life, the dusty streets lined with tyre repair shops, small garages and narrow stalls selling food and hardware and sugar cane and clothes and bright things made from plastic. Dust covers everything with a grey fur; the air is pale with it. Buildings and foliage and vehicles left standing for just a few hours take on a grey monochrome. The only colour seems to come from the many Vietnamese flags that festoon buildings and trees and hang limp and bright in the still air. That and the red and gold hammer and sickle proudly proclaim Vietnam's attachment to Communism.

A brief sidebar on the flag:

Supposedly, the flag was first seen in the uprising against French colonial rule in the South in 1940. The design was attributed to Nguyen Huu Tien, a leader of the uprising who was arrested by the French and executed. (Actions like these were probably the cause of their rioting in the first place. French colonial rule in South East Asia was brutal and the French were universally hated.) According to a poem Tien wrote, the red background represents blood while the yellow foreground represents "the colour of our race's skin"; the five points of the star stand for intellectuals, peasants, workers, traders and soldiers.

Tien's poem reads in part:

... All those of red blood and yellow skin
Together we fight under the nation's sacred flag
The flag is soaked with our crimson blood, shed for the nation
The yellow star is the colour of our race's skin Stand up, quickly!
The nation's soul is calling for us
Intellectuals, peasants, workers, traders and army men
United as a five-pointed yellow star...

Whilst a great story (and terrible poetry - perhaps its subtlety has been lost in the translation), this account has been rejected by Vietnam's Ministry of Culture. More prosaic is the accepted view that the yellow star represents Vietnam while the red ground was inspired by the Communist flag and stands for blood and revolution.

Viet Minh forces used the flag throughout the '40s and, when President Ho Chi Minh proclaimed the Democratic Republic of Vietnam on 5 September 1945, the "bright, five-pointed yellow star" on a "fresh red field" was adopted as the official flag. (Thanks, Wikipedia - well, I think it was Wikipedia.)

In the towns, other bright splashes of colour that manage to resist the coating of dust come from the Chinese goods displayed in many shops, garish reds and blues and golds so bright they make Christmas look boring. The colour alone - that smooth surface gilt and glitter to attract the unwary - proclaims them Chinese and defines them as cheap.

And then there are the huge billboards, brightly-coloured like a child's picture book, showing proudly smiling Vietnamese, men, women and children, clean and fresh-faced and smartly-dressed, farmer and soldier, factory worker and scholar, their arms open as wide as their smiles, giving you all of this success - fields ploughed by phalanxes of modern tractors; productive factories pouring out goods and smoke to be enjoyed by happy workers who offer their labour with a contented smile; students filling their minds with good things; flowers bloom and butterflies flit with colourful abundance. One can almost hear the strains of *The hills are alive...* lilting from each bright and cheerful billboard telling the people just how lucky they really are under Communism.

And, always, somewhere in the background behind each group of joyful workers, the benevolent, smiling face of Uncle Ho, wispy goatee and kind eyes saying, "See, I gave all of this to you - work hard and be happy".

It could have come straight out of the pages of Orwell's 1984.

Yet, behind the bright facade of the posters, all I can see about me is dust and drabness and thin peasant farmers toiling in the land...

I need to buy a coat. As the land rises towards the northern highlands, the temperature drops and I know I will not cope. On the side of a village road I notice clothing on coat hangers, arranged on a rack. I pull over, get off the bike and take a look. There is a jacket. I riffle through the clothing with my fingers, am about to remove the coat and try it on for size when a passing man makes washing motions with his hands and I realise I am fingering someone's laundry.

It's taking time to come to terms with the Vietnamese propensity to regard the street as an extension of their homes.

Later I stop at a village market, an entire block of small stalls, canvas covered, a maze of bright colours and smells - raw meat, spices, fruit, new cotton, live fish gasping their last breaths in large plastic tubs, air bubbling through hose pipes attached to crude pumps powered by car batteries. I am mesmerised by the sheer life of it, the wondrous assault on my senses. I want to absorb myself into it, pause and allow it to take me into its multitudinous riot of living that is so foreign and compelling. Instead of just passing through, I need, for a brief period of time, to become one with it. I buy an orange, sit on a piece of concrete at the edge of some stalls, peel it and eat, the tang of the juice adding another sensory layer to the experience.

Later, reluctantly, I press on, following the road north that parallels the Chinese border just a few kilometres to my right, making for Cao Bang where I will spend the night.

As the afternoon wanes, I stop at a small pavement cafe and ask for tea. Through some lack of understanding I am served, on a tray, a small bowl of black tea and a cup of coffee so thick it's like drinking treacle. (It is only later that I come to realise that, in Vietnam, tea is served as a prelude to anything that is ordered, even coffee.)

The taste lingers in my mouth for the next hour.

* * * * *

So the sergeant dumps this form in front of me and says, "What do you plan to do here, boy?"

And I look him in the eye and I tell him, "Kill gooks."

That's about it, you know? All I wanted to do was kill gooks - kill fucking all of them.

A man with calloused hands

The Karaoke Hotel, Cao Bang, welcomes me after a long day. I am at peace. The roads are alternating rough tar and dirt between small villages, the countryside hilly and wooded, almost devoid of people. Heavy trucks bring goods from China, just a stone's throw to the east.

In the evening I walk through the streets, as is my wont. A group of men sit around a plastic table on the pavement playing a board game, intent and gesticulating; old women sweep litter into neat piles in the gutters to be collected later; a young woman winds coils of copper wire onto reconditioned electric motors using a hand-turned, wooden mechanism. I find a cafe and order coffee. Two old men join me at my table and order tea. They have no English. At another table four young men drink beer. They greet me in Vietnamese and laugh at my incomprehension then summon a teenage girl who speaks halting English and she tries out her handful of words. Her name is Bui Ngayet Auynh - she writes it in my notebook.

A puppy bites my leg and she shoos him away.

The old men take out counters, red and black, marked with Chinese characters, and lay them out on a board roughly cut from a piece of plywood, the playing grid marked in felt pen. They thump the counters down onto the board with crisp clicks and loud exclamations and laughter, dragging on cigarettes held in their wrinkled fingers. The smoke adds an acrid tang to the air.

One of the lads sees me watching, leans over and tells me it's a Chinese game. Being this close to the border, the Chinese influence is everywhere.

Back on the street, I pause to watch a man shape bicycle wheels from rough-cast aluminium profiles. He notices me and invites me in, gesturing to a small table and chair. His son, a mentally defective lad in his early twenties, shakes my hand limply and smiles into my face. He pours me tea and the man gets down a small basket of sweets and offers me one. I take my tea and sit on a piece of cardboard on the pavement, my feet on the step down into his workshop/front room, and watch him work. He holds the rough-cast rim against the side of a foot-long piece of rail track and gently beats it into a curve with a heavy pipe wrapped about with bicycle tube. The muscles on his thin arms are like wires, his hands thick and calloused. He has a gentle, angular face, the yellow skin tanned and leathery.

For a brief moment, into my mind comes unbidden a picture of a pyjamaed Viet Cong, AK47 in hand, making his soundless way through forest shadows. There is something eternal and enduring about this man, a conflicting balance between gentleness and resolve that draws me to him. Momentarily, I feel as if I have brushed against something of the spirit that enabled these people to endure in a war against the most powerful nation in the world.

Lt. Gen. H.G.Moore and J.L.Galloway, in their book "We Were Soldiers Once... and Young", capture the essence of what I am trying to say here:

The Viet Cong and NVA (North Vietnamese Army) or PAVN (People's Army of Viet Nam) are so often in Western reporting on the war treated as nothing more than the Other, the Enemy, referred to as "Gooks" and "Slant-Eyes" in the same way that enemies throughout time have been dehumanised by the use of derogatory terms. Whilst we acknowledge that they too committed atrocities on an equal scale as the American soldiers, they too were human beings with parents who loved and missed them, loved ones who depended on them. In war, the enemy is often reduced to little more than body count. Furthermore, as most of the books written about the war view it from the American perspective and almost all films about the war are American-made, it is inevitable that we get a Western-eyed view of what happened. And as many of these films are of the gung-ho, shoot'em-up genre, our conception of North Vietnamese soldiers as anonymous, suicidal, slant-eyed Gooks attacking American positions has become entrenched in our minds. It is only when we look at the war from the personal accounts of those who fought there, the hardship, loneliness, suffering that took place on both sides that we see it as it really was - a terrible tragedy. And, as is always the case in war, it is the innocent civilians caught in the cross-fire who always suffer most, whose casualties are usually far higher than any of those in uniform, and whose story is so seldom told and for whom few monuments are raised.

Perhaps this brief extract from the jottings in a notebook found in the pocket of a dead North Vietnamese soldier will give a face to the faceless enemy, the slant-eyed Gook of film and fiction:

"Oh, my dear. My young wife. When the troops come home after the victory, and you do not see me, please look at the proud colours. You will see me there, and you will feel warm under the shadow of the bamboo tree."

While I watch, the man checks the rim he has been working on for roundness by fitting it inside a metal bowl. He returns it to the hollow V between the surface and base of the rail and hits it a few more times with the rubber-wrapped pipe, then checks it again for truth inside the metal bowl. When he is happy with its shape, he places it to one side on a pile of completed rims waiting for the fitting of spokes, and reaches for another rim.

I sip my tea, watching him. His actions are automatic, practiced, deft; the effort expended minimal, his hands working as if apart from him. And I realise that this man, for me, now, has given me the "face to the faceless enemy, the slant-eyed Gook of film and fiction..."

Somehow it is easier knowing that we share nothing of each other's language; we do not have to attempt conversation, struggle to find and string together words that catch on the tongue, nor do we have to expend energy attempting to make sense of each other's stumbling effort at communication. In essence, in all that really matters, we understand each other: he knows I am happy just to sit and watch him work, appreciating his industry, the honesty of his toil, the utilitarian nature of the tools he has adapted to craft an artefact from basic casting to functioning wheel that he can sell, adding the value that enables him to feed his family and look after his son. It gives me pleasure to sit quietly and be absorbed for a brief time into the periphery of his life, and know that he is happy that I am there. I have honoured him by my presence, by agreeing to his offer of tea; he has honoured me by serving me tea, by allowing me to sit on a piece of cardboard on his step, one remove from the street outside, enter briefly into the orbit of his life.

Another rim completed and he calls to his son who lumbers over to me and offers me a plastic container of peeled apple slices held in his crooked hands. I select one and he insists that I take another.

Life here, away from the bustle of the city, is so different from the way we live in the West: here work and family are not compartmentalised; the day is not divided into segments - these hours for work and these for play/family time. Work here is often an extension of the home; the street an extension of the workshop. Life goes on. There seem to be no fixed hours. Young children play in the street amongst old men smoking and concentrating on board games; older children share the work of their parents; the TV plays continuously in a corner; a family sits cross-legged and eats; people work... all from rooms that open onto the pavement.

Many is the time when, looking for some place to eat, I have walked past a home where the family is sitting down to a meal and checked myself before walking in and ordering something to eat. Sometimes I am invited in off the street, encouraged to sit down and share tea or food. There is nothing forced about it, nothing to prove. The invitation is an extension of the flow of their lives, a natural expression of their generosity.

How much we have lost as we wall ourselves away from each other, make arbitrary boundaries, treat strangers with suspicion...

A brief next-day reflection:

I cannot speak the language so I must observe. I see a strong yet gentle-faced man toiling into the night, skilled at what he does, using basic, adapted tools, taking a pride in his work, his retarded son cared for and given dignity and responsibility within the bounds of his ability, showing hospitality to a stranger. Their home is utilitarian and clean, nothing showy or garish, no excess - surely this man and his family must have something to teach us in the West. There is no obesity here in this country, no road rage, no drunkenness that I have witnessed so far. The hooting on the roads, annoying for those unaccustomed to it, is just a nudge saying *I'm here!* instead of *Bugger off out of my way, you useless git*. Women are a normal part of life, integrated and involved, not relegated to the back yard, smothered and controlled. There is no hustle, no in-your-face coercion one faces constantly in places like Morocco, Egypt, Gambia.

Whether a society needs this hustle in order to progress, I couldn't judge. Is it better for the individual or society for a trading people to sit passive and apathetic behind the display of their wares and hope that a passer-by will pause and make a purchase or to be out there on the street touting for customers - who can say? Perhaps it's a consequence of the Communist mind-set. For me, as a passer-by, it's far more pleasant not to have to fend off the egregiously insincere, "Hello, my friend, how are you?" calls at every corner.

That energy and motivation certainly drives sales, but does it enhance character?

* * * * *

Right away they told us not to call them Vietnamese. Call everybody gooks, dinks.

Then they told us when you go over in Vietnam, you gonna be face to face with Charlie, the Viet Cong. They were like animals, or something other than human. They ain't have no regard for life. They'd blow up little babies just to kill one GI. They wouldn't allow you to talk about them as if they were people. They told us they're not to be treated with any type of mercy or apprehension. That's what they engraved into you. That killer instinct. Just go away and do destruction.

From "Bloods" by Wallace Terry

Untouched by my passing

The road West into the highlands is good, narrow and winding through deep green bush and ragged banana trees, conical mountains giving perspective to the many small Montagnard villages clustered in the valleys. The steep-sided mountains are terraced, some paddies water-filled and glinting in the sun.

The hill-tribe peoples living in mountainous regions close to the borders of China, Laos and Cambodia were called Montagnards - "highlanders" or "mountain people" - by the French during their attempt at colonising this region. The term was essentially derogatory. Even today, ethnic Vietnamese, who prefer living on the lower coastal plains where rice is more easily grown, refer to the Montagnards as "savages".

Living their subsistence lives in the forest, Montagnards were left in peace, so long as they recognised Vietnamese sovereignty and didn't cause trouble. But the French preferred the cooler climate of the highlands and, as so often happens when little people scratching a living on marginal land that becomes attractive to a more powerful ruler, the hill people were pushed off their patches of land to make way for more lucrative plantations run by the French.

Sadly, during the American War, both sides recruited Montagnard men to fight on their side, mainly as trackers and guides, but also as guerrilla fighters who knew this strategically important area like their back yard, which in a way it was, especially as it was through this area that the Ho Chi Minh Trail made its clandestine way. It is estimated that 200,000 Montagnards were killed during the war. But their suffering did not end when hostilities ceased. After the North Vietnamese took control, many hill people who had fought beside the South Vietnamese and US forces were imprisoned or executed.

Inevitably, these people will lose their identity. One can still see women and children wearing traditional clothing in more remote areas and smoke from their fires often dulls the sky as they find new pieces of virgin forest to slash and burn. Tourism might keep their culture alive a little longer but, as so often happens when back-packer tours to "traditional ethnic villages" become de rigour and photo-snapping tourists by the bus-load flock to gawk at villagers in their "natural" surroundings, it will degenerate into farce with local people dressing up to please the tourists and demanding payment for photographs; then little tourists shops will open selling made-in-China ethnic dolls and plastic models of stilted houses and water buffalo. Women selling tourist tat will start tugging at the sleeves of back-packers and children will call out, *Hey, Meester! Hey, Meester!* on the streets. "Traditional" meals will be served to the bus-tired travellers while small groups of women with bored faces sing to tourists who glance at their watches and wonder how long before the bus leaves and whether there's a party on tonight.

Am I being cynical? I don't think so. Like animals on the Red List, small remnant groups of indigenous people do not survive long when leant on by more powerful civilizations.

I ride slowly, taking in the lives of a people who are oblivious of, and untouched by, my passing.

Wanting to get closer and yet closer, I take an unmarked side track, steep and dirt, emerging through thick clumps of bamboo and banana trees to a small village, the people still living in a by-gone age. Water buffalo, stoop-headed and hairy, make their slow way between the houses, wood-built and raised above the level of the land on stilts, hidden amongst banana and citrus trees and large fish ponds dug from the clay.

I get off the bike and sit next to a partially flooded paddy field. Water trickles along a narrow channel in the dyke edge just below my feet; in the middle of the paddy, a woman, conical hat shading her face, feet gum-booted, controls a buffalo with two pieces of thin cord attached to its nose. The large animal pulls a single-bladed plough that cuts the wet soil clean as a knife and turns it over in glistening folds. I sit quietly as she approaches, ask and receive permission to photograph her.

In a way, I'm sad that I need - want - to take a photograph; it's always an intrusion, a technological barrier between myself and the life being lived in front of me. Just to sit and assimilate this scene with my senses, my thoughts, ought to be enough, something that could have reached out from the mists of pre-history to touch my world.

Sweetly smiling, she turns the large beast with gentle tugs on the cords, making encouraging noises with her mouth, her gum-booted feet squelching deep into the mud. The plough turns upon itself and begins a new cut, clean and precise, the water buffalo moving unhurried and un-driven, its pace as elemental as the land, the rising and falling of the water and these people who inhabit it.

In another field, men and women together hoe furrows in a ploughed field and sow seed by hand.

And I think: It's no wonder the Americans couldn't win their war. There's was a limited intrusion into a land of eternal rhythms, violent and temporal. These people could simply absorb it into themselves, into the land and their bodies, and wait until it passed, as they knew it would. The West functions on an entirely different understanding of time. Their shock and awe was always going to be a temporal thing. A peasant land will always outlast this violence through quiet suffering, retaliation as and when possible, a preparedness to shed blood and lives totally disproportionate to that which we in the West will tolerate - and eventually they will win. As many Americans have said, "We won every battle in Vietnam but lost the war."

* * * * *

The first time I killed somebody up close was when we was tailing Charlie on a patrol somewhere around Danang. It was night. I was real tired. At that time you had worked so hard during the day, been on so many details, you were just bombed out.

I thought I saw this dog running. Because that white pyjama top they wore at night just blend into that funny-coloured night they had over there. All of a sudden, I realised that somebody's runnin'. And before I could say anything to him, he's almost ran up on me. There's nothing I can do but shoot. Somebody get that close, you can't wait to check their ID. He's gonna run into you or stop to shoot you. It's got to be one or the other. I shot him a bunch of times. I had a 20-round clip, and when he hit the ground, I had nothing. I had to reload. That's how many times he was shot.

Then the sergeant came over and took out the flashlight and said, "Goddam. This is fucking beautiful. This is fucking beautiful."

This guy was really out of it. He was like moanin'. I said, "Let me kill him." I couldn't stand the sound he was makin'. So I said, "Back off, man. Let me put this guy out of his misery." So I shot him again. In the head.

He had a grenade in his hand. I caught him just in time.

From "Bloods" by Wallace Terry

A remote land

Later I stop for coffee at some nameless village and realise that I've travelled only 48 of my planned 240ks to Ha Giang where I hope to spend the night. But I am happy and at peace. Time passes slowly here and I have no need to hurry it along. I want to tarry awhile, savour the strong coffee poured over ice, listen to the companionable chirping of birds, unfamiliar voices speaking a foreign tongue on the street outside, children's voices playing...

I am perversely satisfied that there are no tourists here, have been none for the past two days, selfishly want to keep this place to myself. Here it is spotlessly clean, not even a cigarette butt on the street outside. (My, what a filthy nation we are by comparison.)

My host is a Chinese-looking man, heavy set, who is looking after his daughter - two years old, he tells me. She has a packet of sweets and he opens it for her with the instruction, "Just one..."

To one side of the room a brightly-coloured Buddha stands on a small plinth, reflecting the light from his smooth, golden-polished skin; he smiles at the world with a benign plumpness, overlooking the offerings of food - soft drinks, cigarettes, supermarket canned food - that he will never eat, the burned-out spines of long-dead joss sticks poking from a receptacle of sand.

In most homes you will see a Buddha, some with multi-coloured flickering lights making them, with their plastic-gilded veneer and bright colours, the ultimate religious kitsch rivalling only garish statues of Jesus with pulsing neon heart.

Later, reluctantly, I get back on the bike and ride on past small, red-flag-draped towns and villages whose bi-syllabic names are as foreign as the paddy fields and water buffalo and peasants wearing conical hats: Hong Quang, Na Mo, Ma Ran, Thong Nong, Ka Kia, Man Coc, Bang Dong, Hong Tri...

Being so close to the border with China, large trucks dominate the narrow, winding road that makes its way through the mountains. I make sure the muscle-memory of my brain understands the universal truth that four-wheeled vehicles take precedence over puny things with a mere two and whoever is largest will always dictate the terms of engagement on the road.

I must stress that the truck drivers here are not aggressive, just assertive of their God-given right to dominate. If they want to overtake a slower vehicle, they do, no matter who or what is in their way. Of course, they are kind enough to give fair warning of their intentions - an imperative blast on the horn and flashing lights are ample warning that they are heading onto your personal space and you need to get out of the way. And if that means pulling right off the hard shoulder and stopping, then so be it.

That's the way it is here. Get used to it.

The land is beautiful, its remoteness enticing. There are more animals here than people: water buffalo make their ponderous way along the hard shoulder, the grey fluff on their fat stomachs looking soft as a cat's, heads strangely tilted back so that their horns lie flat against their shoulders. Fat-bellied pigs snuffle about, so cute I'd like to take one home as a pet; ducks and fowls scratch and forage near any homestead. It's a land seemingly lost in time. I pass a wooden-wheeled, medieval-looking cart weighed down with bamboo poles as thick as my arm, laboriously pulled by a water buffalo, the Montagnard owner sitting on the load and allowing the beast to make its own way. Roadside stalls selling sugar cane cut into precise lengths by old women, the tall clumps of untrimmed cane behind them reminding me of my youth. For a time I ride alongside the wide, green, slow-flowing Gam River and where the land is steep, soil and rocks have tumbled down onto the road.

Deep in the surrounding bush, stilted Montagnard houses, their wide verandas and open-plan interiors speaking of communal living and restful afternoons lying in strung hammocks. On cleared fields, engine-driven cultivators break up the soil ready for planting and between steep-sided valleys, conical hills meld and smudge into the distance, bush-green and verdant, like mammalian clouds facing the sky.

I stop to take a photograph and step backwards into a six-foot deep drain on the side of the road. Jarred but unhurt, I scramble out, realising how easy it is for life to end. I'm relieved it wasn't deeper or had nasty things at the bottom like Viet Cong punji sticks to impale me or break my bones.

Across the road a hill woman squats in the dust and hacks at a log with a wicked-looking billhook, her teeth worn down and black.

She doesn't notice my fall.

* * * * *

When we passed trough those villages, we really had to watch out for the kids. They would pick up arms and shoot at you. And we had to fire right back.

When we were going out from an operation not very far from Vung Tau, we went through a hamlet we were told was friendly. Quite naturally, you see the women and the children. Never see the men. The men are out conducting the war.

We had hooked up with some army guys, so it was about a company of us. As soon as we got about a half-mile out down the road, we got hit from the rear. Automatic gunfire. It's the women and the children. They just opened up. And a couple of our guys got wasted.

The captain who was in charge of this so-called expeditionary group just took one squad back to the village. And they just melted the whole village. If women and children got in the way, then they got in the way.

From "Bloods" by Wallace Terry

The symmetry of a Japanese Zen garden

Later I pause and sit on the edge of a paddy field, trying to understand their construction and the ageless cycle of rice cultivation that has dominated rural life here for centuries. The afternoon is hot. All around me is the sound of water trickling. To one side a buffalo and her calf crop grass, belly-deep in mud. Their legs make sucking noises when they move.

The soil is fine, a yellow clay easily cut with a plough when wet, leaving an edge crisp and smooth. But when dry, it hardens to the firmness of sandstone, making it ideal for shaping into the terraced walls that hold the water when the paddy fields are flooded prior to planting. Over time, whole mountains have been re-formed into gentle curves that follow the contours and form the flooded paddy fields, bright green with new life, the water glinting and reflecting the sky, creating a landscape so iconic that it has become the defining image of Vietnam that we see in every travel agent's glossy brochure, peasant women wearing conical hats, bent at the waist, planting rice seedlings in neat rows...

Of course, this deep layer of malleable clay enabled villagers to dig tunnels beneath their houses to escape the bombing during the American war. It wasn't long before Viet Cong cadre realised the potential of these personal bomb shelters and encouraged/forced villagers to deepen and extend them to hide and store arms and supplies. If they refused or were not compliant, a few executions for not being supportive of the cause soon changed villagers' minds. Entrances to the tunnels needed to be well hidden because, during the day, South Vietnamese and US soldiers would search for arms caches and evidence that they were supporting the VC. If found, they were killed. South Vietnamese soldiers encouraged/forced villagers to back them during the day, putting up flags and posters on public buildings; the VC dominated the night, re-entering the villages, taking down the flags and replacing them with their own, meeting out punishments to anyone they felt were supporting the Americans or the South until daylight sent them back into the safety of the jungle; then the ARVIN soldiers would return and look for signs of collaboration with the VC and mete out punishment for that. And, sadly, it was the villagers who became the pawns caught in the middle of this bloody game.

Slowly, over a period of decades, these personal bomb-shelter tunnels and hidden chambers excavated out of the firm clay were extended and joined into the network that served the NVA and VC so well during the war and frustrated the Americans when their soldiers continued to be shot by invisible snipers who emerged from hidden entrances to the tunnels, killed and disappeared before they could be found.

(I encourage you to read *When Heaven and Earth Changed Places* by Le Ly Hayslip for a better understanding of the sufferings of rural Vietnamese who were forced to give overt support to both sides during the war. For many years during the conflict the VC dominated the villages by night, the US and ARVIN soldiers controlled them during the day and severe punishment was meted out by both sides for any perceived support of the enemy.)

I look out over the placid fields. There is no sign of the war now, no trace left here. Water trickles past my feet along carefully dug channels, ready to be diverted into paddies by opening up a channel and then, when flooded, closing it again with a plug of clay. Narrow terrace walls in the distance take on the symmetry of a Japanese Zen garden. The water in the paddies is glass-clear; small bubbles rise as trapped air finds its slow way to the surface. Eyes half closed in contentment, the water buffalo and her calf chew grass in the sun, the occasional pull and suck of their footfalls the only sound above the trickle of water.

I am beginning to understand the cultivation of this land, a cycle of the ages. Once the hill slopes have been terraced, clay walls constructed and water channelled from sources higher up the mountain, the land is made ready for planting. To do this, the rock-hard clay has to be broken up and turned into a soup of mud that will hold the roots of the rice plants and cover them with water until the drying-off period before harvest. First a small amount of water is released into the paddy to soften the clay. Then a water buffalo is harnessed to a single plough and gently driven up and down until the whole has been turned over. This clay, the consistency of plasticine, now needs to be turned into soft mud. More water is allowed into the paddy by opening up the wall of the channel at my feet until it looks like a shallow lake. Grass and weeds that have taken root during the fallow period are removed at this time, usually with a wide harrow, home-made from welded reinforcing bar, drawn by a water buffalo. Now men manipulate rotavators through this slurry, with wide paddles on either side driven by single-cylinder engines. A slow and laborious task, this repeated rotavation, around and around each field, the worker up to his knees in glutinous mud, churning the lumps into slurry the consistency of yoghurt. This is left to settle until the mud is firm enough to hold the roots of the seedlings, the water above now clear and still. This planting is a communal affair and often one will see lines of twenty or more women, young and old, stooped and knee-deep in mud, a small tray of seedlings floating on top of the water close within reach, dabbing the seedlings with quick, deft prods, the spacing of the bright green plants even and pleasing to the eye.

Reluctantly I get up from the side of the paddy field and make my way back to the bike. The water buffalo and her calf glance at me, unconcerned.

* * * * *

This other time I had to guard this sergeant, a white guy, on our way to Cambodia. I don't even know how they picked him up. He was busted for raping a Vietnamese woman. His thing was that he just felt that they were animals and didn't deserve to be treated like people.

I was told to give him a weapon in case we get into a fight. I only had one spare weapon, a defective M-79 grenade launcher. It didn't have a safety catch on it , so you couldn't load it unless you were ready to fire. I told him not to load it unless we made contact. He loaded it anyway. He was sitting slightly behind me with the weapon lying across his lap, facing towards me.

We went across a bump, and it went off, just an inch behind my back, and exploded in the woods somewhere.

I turned the .50 around on him. It didn't turn round as far as I wanted it. So I got up out of the track, pulled my M-16 and told him to get off the track. Just leave. He wouldn't move, so I kicked him off.

From "Bloods" by Wallace Terry

Hi Giang and the abuse of medieval instruments

By late evening I reach Hi Giang and find somewhere to stay. Outside my room an old Montagnard couple, small even by Vietnamese standards, crouch on the pavement and grill cobs of maize and sweet potatoes over a charcoal fire. The smell of charred maize mixes with the sweet perfume of joss sticks in the evening air.

Across the road a dozen cats are being slowly and methodically tortured. The sound is so discordant and overpowering that I am drawn to discover what it is that could possibly create such a dreadful noise and why nobody has called the police. I walk along the pavement towards the sound. It seems there is a cultural thing happening; tables are neatly laid out and important-looking men with note pads in front of them look suitably serious. Behind them a group of young men, dressed in black and with white King Foo headbands wait for someone in charge to say, "Let the proceedings begin..." or something similar.

And behind them, the origin of this cacophony, a local quartet is abusing medieval-looking instruments. Had they been used in the manner of their design, the noise might not have been quite so overpowering, but amplified to the extent that the ears of passing pedestrians bleed somehow spoils the effect.

I walk away to a quieter part of town, looking for somewhere that will serve food. Not having eaten since the roll and strawberry jam I consumed for my breakfast has left me a little shaky. Or maybe it's just the long hours riding through the mountains; or the jarring my body received when I stepped backwards and fell into the hole. At my age, disappearing down a 6-ft hole is somewhat unsettling.

I find a secluded street; it is dark except for the fairy-tale light of a hundred multi-coloured Chinese lanterns suspended from overhanging trees. The effect is magical and reminds me of those late-evening mass hot-air balloon launches they sometimes stage near Bristol, the fairy light from the gas flares illuminating the balloons from within.

There are a number of places that look like intimate restaurants with small groups of people gathered round a communal table, chopsticks in hand, but I hesitate to enquire in case I intrude upon a family eating their evening meal; by now I have come to understand how, unlike our walled-off lives, Vietnamese families often expose their domestic arrangements to the full view of passers-by in the street.

In the end I cross a bridge over a fast-flowing river and find a barge tethered to the bank serving delicious food - and beer. I eat with chopsticks and think I am doing well until a kindly old man sitting at another table comes to my aid with a spoon and an understanding smile.

On the telly Tottenham are playing Arsenal, the chanting from the spectators like a friendly voice from home.

*****

Towards the end of my tour, people started getting very hostile towards each other, because it was getting late in the war. And there were a lot of drugs around. And a lot of people were taking them. The Communists were making sure the American soldiers got them. And others were making sure drugs were available, because they could make a lot of money. Drugs took a great toll on all soldiers.

Some guys were choked to death in their sleep, because they drank too much alcohol or were taking drugs. Some ODed. They were mainly not really smoking grass so much anymore, but taking "number tens", which are something like Quaaludes, and speed. And that was devastating, taken together. Of course, there was the scag. And whether you smoked it or snorted it, you got really fucked up.

One night, two white guys were playing this game in a bunker along the perimeter checkpoint as you leave the base camp at An Khe on the way to Qui Nhon. They had been taking speed and number tens. So they began to play with this grenade. Taking the pin out and putting it back in. They did it for a time, until one of them made a mistake and dropped the pin. When he found it, he was so nervous he couldn't quite get it in, and the grenade exploded. It killed him. And his partner was critically injured.

From "Bloods" by Wallace Terry

Iron bars and bloody teeth

The road descends from the mountains and, once more, I am reunited with traffic and the clustering of human beings. It's not long before I yearn for the mountains again, the crisp, cool air, the cleanness of it. Here in this corridor of writhing humanity from Viet Quang towards Sa Pa it is too loud, too noisy. The land is smeared with living, with too many people trying to share the same crowded space. The colours are too bright - reds and yellows, gold too where cheap Chinese goods are displayed for sale. Even the flowers are too bright. Florists line the streets, carefully prepared bouquets on display, but they try too hard; the lily is gilded until it becomes plastic and tawdry. A rose is just not rosy enough here - it has to be spangled with glittery stuff; green fronds are not green enough - the bouquets are set off with lavishly garish pink and purple and green tissue paper so that the flowers themselves take on that blowsy cheap tartness of the pink and blue magazine covers aimed at women of a certain class with a taste for the sordid affairs of celebrities. Vietnamese weddings, celebrated with such public enthusiasm on all main streets, sadly share this same tawdry affectation; pantomime celebrations, overly bright, with plastic flowers and loudspeakers turned up to full volume.

Is this something they've picked up from us? I'm sure that, in the old days of Vietnam, weddings were never celebrated in this ghastly way and flowers were allowed to be... well, flowers.

Riding through a smallish town whose name I didn't catch, on the opposite side of the road I notice a large pig in distress. The sight disturbs me so I turn back. A female pig, black and as large as a small pony, has been trussed into a cigar-shaped cage made of welded round-bar, encasing her so tightly that she cannot move. It wraps her up, cages her, a torturous Iron Maiden with its living burden lying prostrate and helpless on the pavement between the feet of pedestrians who make their way around her, unconcerned. Her legs have been bent and the metal rods press them into her flesh; there is blood and saliva running out of her mouth.

Seeing that she does not move, with a sense of relief I conclude that she is dead; they have slaughtered her and pressed her into this cage to facilitate transport.

But then I notice that she is breathing. And while I watch, she struggles in little spasms and cries out, all that the constricting cage will allow. She has taken an iron bar into her mouth and her teeth are bloody with the biting of it. While I watch, she gnaws at the iron, as thick as my thumb, trying to bite her way free; more blood and saliva flows from her mouth.

The owner of this atrocity sees me looking, approaches with a smile and speaks to me. In my helplessness I shout at him, pointing, venting my anger and my hurt at his cruelty.

He doesn't understand.

Sad and impotently angry, filled with a sense of self loathing towards the human race, I get back on my bike and ride away, still shouting and gesticulating at the man who observes my departure with a look of bewilderment on his face.

And as I leave this suffering creature behind, I attempt to rationalise my feelings. In many societies animals are treated as commodities, senseless beasts whose sole function is to provide meat or power or protection. We've all seen the disturbing photographs of donkeys beaten and abused; cats squashed into cages so tightly they cannot move; dogs strung up, flogged and then skinned alive before slaughter; grinning idiots clutching high-powered rifles and holding up the heads of wild animals they have shot; young men, waist-deep in bloody water, hacking porpoises to death. I suppose I would need to add here, too, the shocking things we do to our fellow human beings in the name of religion or politics or whatever.

Is it that some of us have evolved to a higher moral plane? Is our anthropomorphising our animals a good thing or is it a sign of a degenerate people who dress up dogs in human clothes and place diamond-studded collars around their necks and feed them steak while most of the human race goes to sleep each night hungry? We in the West no longer beat our donkeys to death when they can't carry the impossible loads we place on their backs; we don't skin dogs alive to tenderise their flesh through the internal secretions of their own distress; we as a nation - well, most of us - react with horror at animal cruelty, legislate over the destruction of the habitat of newts and the quality of life of chickens.

This, surely, is a good thing, an example of civilized behaviour.

Should I have shouted into the face of this man who was merely doing what has been done in his country for generations? The pig needed to be carried to market - probably on the back of a scooter. It needed to be alive. How do you transport a large pig from your farm into town when your only mobility is a scooter? You immobilise the pig. And how do you immobilise a large pig other than trapping it into a sausage-shaped metal cage that stops it leaping about and causing an accident?

Perhaps it is my visceral fear of confined spaces, a claustrophobia that sometimes soaks my sheets at night; perhaps it is my love of living things - I catch bees trapped against window panes and set them free; do the same for spiders, allow wasps to nest on the veranda and accept the possibility of their stings as an acceptable quid pro quo; in

Africa I would catch snakes that invaded our house and set them free at the bottom of the garden with an encouraging word. They are delicate, gentle creatures all and, I believe, have just as much right to life on this precious planet as we do. Our lives are enriched by theirs.

Does this make me a better person than the peasant farmer and his trussed pig? And have I the right to judge?

I try to push these thoughts aside and focus on the landscape through which I am travelling. I have come again upon an area of urban sprawl; not a city or large town - rather a succession of villages that blend one with another using the road as their focal point, their open-fronted shops benefiting from the passing hoards. Yet, through this maelstrom of humanity, nature continues to burst through, irrepressible. There is a greenness deep-down things, as Hopkins observes, flaming out like shining from shook foil. Banana leaves shake their ragged elephant ears in the gentle breeze, darkly green; sugar cane rustles in dry whispers; bamboo, so tall you can almost feel it growing, bends over the road; trees with leaves the size of cats absorb light and give off a warm fug of watery transpiration. There is a wetness in the air...

* * * * *

So this same captain came up to me. He stared at me. I had this chicken in my hand.

He said, "Don't cut that chicken up."

He wants it saved for the eggs, I guess.

"You cut that chicken's head off, I'm a have you court-martialled."

I bent over and I bit the chicken head off and spit it in his face. And he throwed up.

From "Bloods" by Wallace Terry

A chicken leg and communicating without words

Needing, once again, the healing balm of the mountains sans people, I take a small track that leads me vaguely in the right direction towards Sa Pa. I need to smell wood-smoke instead of diesel fumes for a while, to feel the road rough and pot-holed and undulating beneath my tyres, in contact with the land again. I pass through a forested area where logging is the main activity. Cut logs are stripped of their bark and sliced into sheets of veneer two mm thick and laid out in the sun to dry. Newly cut, the wood is smooth and white like the skin of young girls and it perfumes the air with the sweetness of its sap.

The road deteriorates rapidly, becoming dirt, its surface chopped up by the wheels of heavy logging trucks, wet and slippery.

In a cafe I am invited to sit at a table with five old men. One pours tea for me into a small round bowl. He has the hands of a labourer, gnarled and damaged, the nails long and thick.

(It is of interest to note that, throughout Vietnam, it seems to be the accepted practice for men to leave one nail long, often the pinkie finger. I wasn't able to ask anyone local why and checking on the Internet threw up a number of insensitive responses by so-called travellers who did little more than express their disgust. Other than for the ease of scratching some of our more inaccessible orifices, more reasoned explanations seem to suggest that the custom derives from China where it is considered more auspicious when the pinkie is at least longer than the distal knuckle on the ring finger; another plausible explanation is to indicate that the owner of long nails belongs to a higher caste whose members do not soil their hands with manual labour. I am quite sure that there are more intelligent people than myself who could give an authoritative reason.)

The five old men and I sit on wooden benches in front of a low table. They take turns to smoke a *Dieu Cay*, the metre-long pipe made from a length of bamboo commonly smoked by the older men in Vietnam. Water in the bottom filters and cools the smoke and makes a pleasant gurgling sound when a smoker places his mouth over the opening and sucks. Only a small pinch of tobacco is placed in the mouth of the pipe so the smoking becomes something of a ritual, like the pouring of tea.

They offer me the pipe but I shake my head, pointing to my lungs and making a face. They laugh and continue passing the pipe from hand to hand. We drink our tea in companionable silence, one of the men topping up my bowl whenever I drain it.

Suddenly one of the men gets up and makes his way to a very out-of-date soccer World Cup poster that has been tacked to a wall. On it are the flags of all the countries involved. He points to the Vietnamese flag and then indicates himself. Then he invites me to show them where I come from and I get up and point to the Union flag. They clap their hands and smile and one calls out, "Manchester United!" - the universal language of football.

Once again we have found a way of communicating without words.

Time to move on. I take out my wallet to pay but they wave me away then gather round as I ready the bike, exclaiming at the GPS.

Later I stop at a Montagnard settlement, looking for a meal. I approach a house hidden deep within the gloom of trees and tall groves of bamboo that lean and sway in the breeze; ducks waddle between seats made from sawn-off logs. An old man welcomes me, shakes my hand. His wife is washing her hair under a tap covered by a palm-frond-thatched roof held up by thick bamboo poles. The ducks waddle over to investigate the pool of water about her feet and she shoos them away. A young girl, about fifteen, wearing a dirty t-shirt, approaches me, greets me with a delightful laugh. Her plump baby plays on his own in the dirt.

I gesture for food, a question mark on my face, and she shows me some noodles. I nod. The old man invites me to sit on a wooden bench next to him. I have my notebook and pen on the table. He picks up my glasses and puts them on, then takes up my notebook and flicks through it, shaking his head in incomprehension.

The young girl holds up a chicken leg and asks with her eyebrows if this will be acceptable. Again I nod. She cuts the meat off the leg with a cleaver then boils the pieces of meat in a pot over a charcoal fire. When the meat is done, she scoops it into a bowl of noodles, adds sliced spring onions then pours the broth from the pot over the noodles and gives it to me with some wooden chopsticks. She goes out back behind the house and picks green leaves that she serves me in a bowl then unwraps some toilet paper as a serviette.

I eat in the shaded ground floor of the wooden stilted house. The upper part, the living quarters, is large and open, thatched. It looks cool. There are no windows, just openings in the woven, palm-frond walls; inside I can see the large wooden poles protruding through the floor and holding up the roof. Hammocks have been strung between the poles. I want to ask whether they will show me their home but feel it would be an intrusion so I don't.

Suddenly I am not sure whether this is an eating-house or have I just walked off the road into someone's home and asked for food. There is nothing to suggest it either way. I wonder to myself what we in the West would think (or do) if a foreigner turned up at our front door unannounced, made himself comfortable in the front room and gestured for food.

When I have finished, the old man drags himself off his stump and returns with a bottle of homemade spirit in an orange-juice bottle. He pours two glasses, hands me one and we down the spirit together. He offers me another but I indicate the bike and make crashing gestures. He understands. But my drinking with him he treats as an honour and he takes both my hands in his and looks intently into my face before allowing me to leave.

* * * * *

I used to think that I wasn't affected by Vietnam, but I been livin' with Vietnam ever since I left. You just can't get rid of it. It's like that painting of what Dali did of the melting clocks. It's a persistent memory.

I remember most how hard it was to just shoot people.

I remember one time when three of our people got killed by a sniper from this village. We went over to burn the village down. I was afraid that there was going to be shootin' people that day, so I just kind of dealt with the animals. You know, shoot the chickens. I mean I just couldn't shoot no people. I don't know how many chickens I shot. But it was a little pig that freaked me out more than the chickens. You think you gonna be shootin' a little pig, it's just gonna fall over and die. Well, no. His little guts be hangin' out. He be just squiggling around and freakin' you out.

See, you gotta shoot animals in the head. If we shoot you in your stomach, you may just fall over and die. But an animal, you got to shoot them in the head. They don't understand that they supposed to fall over and die.

From "Bloods" by Wallace Terry

Harvesting sand

The beaten-up road ends. I ride fast along smooth tar following a large tributary of the Red River; the riding is mindless, characterless, made worse by the many heavy trucks on the road crawling at walking pace around hair-pin bends. I watch as the local drivers play Russian Roulette with their cars. It's not a restful experience. A mad person just in front of me decides to take his life in his hands and overtake a truck on a blind corner only to meet another car coming the other way. I expect the blowing of horns and fists being shaken; instead, both cars, nose to nose, stop and wait until the truck has lumbered past, creating space for the suicidal driver to slot in behind again.

No finger pointing, recriminations, raised voices; just a quiet acceptance... wait for the road to clear, carry on with life.

It's a great way to live.

For a while now, the road has been following this river, fast flowing and deep. I have noticed some metal boats, forty-fifty foot long, anchored low in the water doing something industrious. When I come across two more, I feel the need to investigate. Although the road has been constructed a good forty foot above the water, I find a place where I can scramble down to the river's edge and make my way over boulders and through underbrush to where one of the boats is anchored. The other boat is a short way up river.

As with all machinery in the more remote regions, these boats are starkly utilitarian and massively over engineered. There is no paint, no decoration, just bare welded metal, thick and heavy. On the deck, four large motors, one in the stern to drive a long propeller shaft, the other three attached to pumps. A small section of the stern has been covered with a curved roof of corrugated iron held in place by bamboo poles. Wet clothes hang on ropes to dry; everything else is open to the elements. The engines are old, single-cylinder thumpers that billow smoke and dribble oil. A crank handle lies in oily water on the metal deck. A crew of three, bare foot and stripped to the waist, work the pumps. One sees me and waves.

At first I think they might be prospecting for alluvial diamonds but the reality is more mundane: river sand. The boats are manoeuvred into position using the engine and long bamboo poles then anchored or tethered to the bank. Thick reinforced rubber hoses are lowered to the riverbed and the pumps are started. The pipes are old, holes blocked and strapped with plastic and tape, held in place by roughly made bamboo trestles and tied to the edge of the boat with rope. Sand and water are sucked from the riverbed and roughly sieved into the hold. The hull, incredibly strong, is nothing more than a large, shaped metal container for sand. Everything necessary for living and working the boat is on deck, including a small stove and boiler heated by a wood fire. The men continue to fill the hull of the boat in front of me until its gunwale and deck are inches *below* the level of the water; I expect to see it begin to sink but a metal lip, nine inches high, has been welded around the open hatch and only this keeps the boat from sinking. The men are unconcerned. They splash about the flooded deck in their bare feet, the boat apparently disappearing under the water as I watch, continuing to pump sand and water into the already full hold.

I point to the water lapping just inches from the raised edge of the hold and call out, "Your boat's going to sink!"

The man smiles and shakes his head.

One shouts and the pump engine is switched off. Suddenly all is quiet and I can hear the lapping of water, the conversation of the men. They take hold of the long bamboo poles, loosen the ropes securing the boat to the bank and punt the heavy boat a short way down stream to where I notice pipes have been laid up the bank. They secure the boat, connect up the pipes and begin pumping the sand, mixed with water, onto the edge of the road where it is piled, ready to be carted away by trucks.

Sad to leave this scene of rural industry, I clamber up the bank to where my bike is parked and continue on my way.

* * * * *

In the rear sometimes we get a grenade, dump the gunpowder out, break the firing pin. Then you'll go inside one of them little bourgeois clubs. Or go in the barracks where the supply guys are, sitting around playing bid and doing nothing. We act real crazy. Yell out, "Kill all y'all motherfuckers." Pull the pin and throw the grenade. And everybody would haul ass and get out. It would make a little pop sound. And we would laugh. You didn't see anybody jumpin' on them grenades.

One time in the field, though, I saw a white boy jump on a grenade. But I believe he was pushed. It ain't kill him. He lost both his legs.

From "Bloods" by Wallace Terry

Sapa - feeling alone and old

As the sun begins to set, I reach the town of Lao Cai, sharing a border with China, then turn south, climbing steeply to 1400m until I reach Sapa, tourist magnet of the north and close to Phan Si Pan, Vietnam's highest mountain.

This area is very much the preserve of the hill people, Montagnards who can be seen walking along the streets wearing traditional clothes, mainly black and decorated with colourful embroidery.

I find a pleasant hostel and head out to walk the streets. Backpackers congregate in cafes and street eating-houses, drinking beer and sharing experiences. They all speak English although their accents and features bear testimony to the shrinking borders of our global village. I don't attempt to join them; for a brief moment I become conscious of my age. Let the young and beautiful fraternise with their own kind, although a part of me hopes they will see me and call out, invite me into the warm familiarity of their laughter and their drinking, their languid sharing of experiences still bright with the newness of discovery.

They don't and I walk on, feeling alone and old.

Later on the street, I recognise a familiar face: it is Anna from the Czech Republic who shared the bus with me from the airport to Hanoi city centre on my first day in Vietnam. She is with a German girl. A brief hesitation and then she recognises me. We chat briefly and then move on, travellers passing in the night.

A street vendor offers me duck feet and a suspicious looking pale sausage to be cooked on a charcoal burner but I decline. I look for somewhere more salubrious to eat. Most establishments vending food are of the street variety, small plastic chairs arranged on the pavement and one pot simmering over a charcoal burner, the kind where you sit down and are given a bowl of watery noodles and whatever happens to be in the pot.

I walk past. I have become tired of noodles.

Later I come across a cafe with a picture of a piece of fried chicken nestled on a bed of salad, colourful and fresh and piquant. I sit down, point to the picture and give the thumbs up. Yes, I'll have that, please. And a 30p can of beer - horrible stuff but take it or leave it, it's all they've got. A short while later I am presented with half a chicken on a plate.

I point to the picture, prod the bed of fresh salad with an importunate finger and mime a question mark. The young lady shrugs and says haltingly, "Not got."

The chicken is crispy and good but must have spent much of its scrawny life attempting to escape dogs and trucks and hungry peasants intent on slaughter. We in the West have become so used to the flesh of our poultry having the consistency of butter. I had to put my foot on this one to break its leg sinews; eating the flesh was like chewing on a piece of cheap steak. Boy, that chicken had muscles.

Better than noodles, though.

The next day I fill up with petrol and head up the long Dto Tram Ton Pass, following a good but narrow road switch-backing up and over the Hoang Lien Mountains, the air hazy with mist and the blue smoke of bush fires which can be seen burning along the high ridges. This high up it is cold, especially as I am wearing my wet clothes from last night's washing which are reluctant to dry at this altitude.

I pass Montagnard women making their way into Sapa, their small stature, distinctive clothing and black cloth gaiters identifying them long before I am able to see their features.

The Chinese influence here is still strong, many of the inhabitants having left China as refugees fleeing from regional conflicts over the centuries and settling in Vietnam. They are not always welcomed, especially after China's periodical attempts at invasion over the years. Like the Montagnards, people of Chinese origin are often looked at with suspicion and distrust by traditional ethnic Vietnamese.

Yet the Vietnamese themselves are not at one with each other. Despite the years of living in a unified state, there is still tension between north and south, the Communist leanings of the north not sitting well with those living in the more liberal south. The bitterness left after years of fighting on opposite sides during the American War, the atrocities perpetrated by both sides and the vindictive policies that the northern victors imposed on their fellow citizens in a supposedly unified Vietnam after the collapse of the south have never been forgotten. Few who were alive during that time can forget the mass exodus of the Vietnamese "boat people", driven from their homeland after the war ended.

This is a country still trying to find itself. Although signs of Communism are to be seen everywhere - the red flag with gold star fluttering over nearly every building and fishing boat, the hammer and sickle displayed on every propaganda poster - Vietnam, like Russia and China, is slowly opening up and joining the rest of the world, welcoming tourists, beginning to embrace democracy and an open market, leaving behind the more restrictive practices of the past. Very few North Koreas now exist in this world, thank goodness.

* * * * *

I remember February 20. Twentieth of February. We went to this village outside Duc Pho. Search and destroy. It was suppose to have been VC sympathisers. They sent fliers to the people telling them to get out. Anybody else there, you have to consider them as a VC.

It was a little straw-hut village. Had a little church at the end with this big Buddha. We didn't see anybody in the village. But I heard movement in the rear of this hut. I just opened up the machine gun. You ain't wanna open the door, and then you get blown away. Or maybe they booby-trapped.

Anyway, this little girl screamed. I went inside the door. I'd done already shot her, and she was on top of the old man. She was trying to shield the old man. He looked like he could have been about eighty years old. She was about seven. Both of them was dead. I killed an old man and a little girl in the hut by accident.

I started feeling funny. I wanted to explain to someone. But everybody was there, justifying my actions, saying, "It ain't your fault. They had no business there." But then I just - I ain't wanna hear it. I wanted to go home then.

It bothers me now. But so many things happened after that, you really couldn't lay on one thing. You had to keep going.

From "Bloods" by Wallace Terry

Just trust me, mate

My little 125 struggles up the steep Dto Tram Ton Pass but once we peak and head down the other side we speed up and wear a little rubber off the sidewalls. A thick mist billows up from the river far below, blown by a cold wind over a landscape greened to the horizon by forest.

Two peasant women crouch beside a small moped, peering at the rear wheel. I turn back and offer to help. One points to a nail protruding from the side of a very bald tyre. The other is phoning someone using a pink mobile so I push aside my manly intentions and continue on my way. In a country with 37 million motorcycles, someone will have it repaired in a jiffy.

Whilst nowhere near the madness of Hanoi traffic, the main road is still unpleasantly clogged but I have become reasonably tolerant now, understanding the un-logic that underpins the movement of vehicles; I now feel fairly comfortable picking my way through and avoiding collisions. But my tolerance is somewhat stretched when, about midday, I am almost taken out by a youth on a scooter overtaking a bus that is overtaking a truck on a blind corner. He does have the grace to smile at me, though, as I take emergency evasive action, bumping over rocks and loose soil on the side of the road.

Tired of this traffic, I study the map looking for alternatives. I decide to forgo the "Northern Loop" that Lonely Planet recommends for the "adventurous traveller" and take instead a smaller road that makes its way through the mountains south. The road I am on is too cluttered with trucks and cars, too nice. I want to feel the ground beneath my tyres again, smell the smoke from cooking fires, feel the vegetation encroaching onto the road, get lost a little. There are no towns of any note until Nt. Tran Pho about 400 ks to the south but that's the way I prefer it. Once Lonely Planet suggests that this is the route to follow, I have a tendency to want to keep away. It's not long before backpackers clutching guide books and bottles of spring water begin frequenting the place and souvenir stands appear on the roadside with young men calling out, "Hello, my friend - " as you pass. It's as if the very fact of being mentioned in Lonely Planet is the beginning of the inevitable downward slide towards becoming no longer lonely. And it is my experience that travelling through lonely places is usually the preserve of travellers, not tourists.

Petrol won't be a problem. Where there are vehicles there will always be petrol available, even if it's in bottles stored in a dusty shed.

Accommodation? If necessary, I can always sleep on the side of the road or knock on the door of a Montagnard stilted house. These generous people would not turn me away and it would be easy to leave behind on the bed what it would have cost me to stay at a boarding house if they refused payment.

I turn off the main road and, in a small village, see a table under a corrugated iron lean-to with eggs in a basket. I stop and point. A woman with pale olive skin wearing a loose skirt, blouse and thongs on her feet brings me tea and, while I wait for my eggs to fry, offers me half an apple, peeled. Just in front of me on the roadside an old Mama San wearing a conical hat tied under her chin with a red piece of cloth cuts the skins off sticks of sugar cane with a wickedly sharp machete. She catches my eye and offers me some. I nod. She asks me to hold one end of a six-foot length of cane while she whacks off a piece and I am fearful of my fingers. However, she is deft and I hold my piece of sugar cane, all fingers intact, and gnaw and suck, gnaw and suck, juice dripping off my chin onto the ground as memories of my youth come flooding back. I grew up in Natal, South Africa, with vast sugar plantations within metres of our back yard. The fields of cane became our playground and, whenever we felt like it, we would break off a piece, strip the skin with our teeth and gnaw the sweet fibre, sucking the juice and spitting out the masticated bits as we walked between the rustling cane, always bare foot, enjoying a freedom mostly lost to many of today's children.

I eat my fried eggs under the shade of the corrugated iron, the sound of the village going on about me, drink the slightly bitter, smoky black tea, my fingers sticky with juice. When I come to pay I discover three million Dong tucked away in a zippered compartment in my wallet which I didn't know I had. *Three million!* I had wondered why my money seemed to be disappearing more quickly than planned. I am rich and celebrate by buying two boiled eggs for my lunch, which I tuck into a pocket.

I press on, the road narrow and remote, winding through the mountains, thinning forest disappearing into the morning haze. I am not quite sure where I am. There are few road signs and all bear no resemblance to what is shown on my map. My GPS indicates a maze of small roads with occasional names that don't match up with anything. But this is fine. I am heading south and that's all I need to know. There are very few vehicles on the road and the land is mostly unpopulated; just the occasional Montagnard stilted house, nestling inside small copses of bamboo, their neat fields of rice and greens glinting in the sun, a few pot-bellied pigs sunning themselves on the road and banana trees with their cool, dark green leaves.

It is very hot but as long as I keep moving the flow of air keeps me cool. When I do stop on the roadside, the air presses against me, warm and damp from the surrounding forest. Occasionally

I come across a man walking along the road, trousers - always black - rolled up to the calf, bare foot, white button-down shirt open at the neck. It's like a uniform.

My little bike is going well. Lately I seem to be on a downward trajectory where bikes are concerned: four trips on a 500cc; then, last year to Central Asia I downsized to a DR350; now I'm riding a 125. Perhaps in my old age I'll be riding a 50cc postie bike to remote destinations. At least I can still pick them up when they fall over.

Afternoon comes and I'm still "lost". Of course, lost in a relative sense only because you can't be lost if you have no destination. I stop in the sultry heat off the road and once again consult the map and my GPS, searching for just a single corresponding name so I can pinpoint my position. It's not a problem; I'm perfectly happy, but it would be good to know that I'm heading in the right direction.

At last I find a town 397ks south in the direction I am supposed to be heading, punch it in and ask my GPS to take me there. The lady says, "Sure, Boss -" and leads me almost immediately onto a narrow road called, according to my GPS, "16", that takes me high into the mountains to 900 metres. There's no one around, just me and my little bike, the mountains and the forest so, after a while I stop and ask, politely, whether my GPS lady knows where she's going. A little hurt, she says, "Just trust me, mate," in a snippy sort of voice so I do and for two delightful hours I have the road and the mountains entirely to myself; not another vehicle, not even one of those ubiquitous, annoying scooters that seem to be around every corner (usually on the wrong side) in this country.

This, I think to myself, is how travel is supposed to be. This is why I am here...

Later we reach a small town where I fill up with fuel and continue along a slightly wider road, fairly empty of traffic, that my GPS helpfully calls "road" - just in case at some point I need to know.

The heat has become even more oppressive. On the side of the road I see a strange contraption, some umbrellas for shade and the usual assembly of dusty plastic chairs.

Hoping for something cool to drink, I turn around to investigate and am rewarded with a glass of freshly squeezed sugar-cane juice that I share with a congregation of friendly and persistent bees. It has a sweet, earthy flavour.

Finally, as the sun sets behind the mountains, I make it to Son La. I still don't know how I got here. I will try to make it to the coast tomorrow...

Later that evening in a restaurant, a heavy-set man with a round face and pendulous ear lobes, somewhat reminiscent of Buddha, insists I join a group of men at their table. There are six of them, all in their late twenties, of Chinese origin, judging by their size and the shape of their faces. I order some food but they insist I share theirs, repeatedly encouraging me to eat by taking small pieces of meat and other delicacies from the table and dropping them into my bowl.

I am beginning to understand just a little of community life amongst these generous people. There is, in the West, an insularity about the way we live our lives exhibited even in the mundane task of eating. When we partake of a meal, we are each given a plate of food. It is ours, no one else's; we eat it - or not. There is no sharing. Leftovers from each plate are scraped into the bin or fed to family pets.

Not so here.

In Vietnam, it is all about sharing; it's a communal thing. On the table are placed a number of dishes. In front of each person, a small bowl that needs to be constantly re-filled. Everyone seated around the table shares the food that has been provided. There is nothing of the: This is my plate of food, that is yours.

And it enables, as I witnessed, people sharing the meal with you to select choice pieces and place them in your bowl as a gift, the conferring of an honour or blessing.

Amongst us there are, once again, no mutually understandable words, but the gestures communicate all that is needed to be said. I am feted, welcomed, made to feel special. The evening, I come to understand, is a celebration of the man's birthday and I become absorbed into the camaraderie of their group. Later, lethal looking vodka is produced in 500ml plastic cool drink bottles and we toast one another, all together, two by two, the emptied glass immediately refilled, hands shaken all round after each toast. Then a young lady arrives and she needs to be toasted in turn... and again and yet again.

Normally a one-drink man, I believe I consumed six or so glasses of this lethal brew and, strangely, my ability to manipulate the chopsticks improved after each toast.

When my benign, round-faced host suggests that the young lady fancies me and - judging by the gestures he makes with his hands - would like to have sex with me, I decide it is time to take my leave.

Much later, my lips somewhat numb, I manage to extricate myself from the web of their generosity and bid them farewell.

I realise that much of my writing on this trip has involved eating and the people who have shared meals with me or prepared meals for me but, when travelling alone, it is the sharing of meals with strangers that allows one to enter into the lives of the people through whose country one is travelling. The lone stranger is far more likely to be invited to join local people than a group. Like-minded travellers tend to stick together, eating and sharing with each other the experiences of their day.

And it is the indigenous people rather than the landscape that gives character to a country, beautiful as it might be.

How generous and welcoming the Vietnamese people have been to me and how much I have come to realise that we, in the West - by our insularity, by the walls, literal and metaphorical, we build around ourselves and those we call our own - have lost something precious that is still retained in some cultures in this world, most often amongst the poor.

*****

There was this sergeant who got medivaced out. He'd been lost for a couple of days, lying in a canal, up to his neck in water, waiting for someone to come back for him. His one arm was all fucked up and he was full of frags. I cut off his sleeve and nearly throwed up. All there was left was bone and some muscle. It was full of maggots. He was pretty out of it by then so he didn't see me trying not to puke.

I just wanted to go home. I've had enough of this shit.

A scene from the Middle Ages

The road south towards Thanh Hoa and the coast is, once again, clogged with traffic and urban sprawl and I navigate my way through a constantly moving maze - scooters weave in front of me in a noisy filigree; trucks cut a straight path, hooting and asserting their right to own the road, nudging us lesser beings aside with flashing lights and stridently sounding horns.

The road follows the Nam Pan and Nam San rivers and at last, for a time, we break free from the smog and clutter of people and industry. I pass children swimming in the river, playing on rafts made from lengths of bamboo lashed together; water buffalo who doze on the roadside, their heads tilted back, ruminating; women in ragged lines who stoop, calf-deep in mud, to plant achingly green rice seedlings with deft, mechanical prods. The road climbs into mountains shrouded in mist, their steep sides green with plantations of ragged-leaved bananas and mature mango trees.

I pause alongside a paddy field, the sun warm against my shoulders, and allow myself again to be drawn into the lives of these hard-working people, still an outsider, still one who observes from the edges of their lives, but a little closer than when merely riding past.

In the near distance, a man walks behind a water buffalo. He wears gum boots and his feet sink calf-deep into the mud at each step. The paddy field has been ploughed before and is now inundated, the mud having taken on a yoghurt-like consistency from many ploughings, rotavations and, now, a final sieving with a home-made harrow, two metres wide, with long metal prongs that comb through the mud, breaking up any remaining clods, removing the last traces of grass and weed and mixing the mud to that fine tilth that allows the rice seedlings to flourish. The buffalo plods closer, its massive weight thrusting its legs deep at every step. It seems unconcerned; makes its slow way towards me, drawing the heavy, many-pronged metal rake as if unaware of the burden, pausing every now and then to stare then, with the encouragement of a little flick of the cords attached to its nostrils, it takes another step and then another, the sucking of its hooves coming clear in the still air. There is timelessness about the scene that takes me back hundreds of years, thousands; I could be watching a scene from the Middle Ages.

The man and his ox pass me and he looks up and smiles.

In a nearby field women are planting rice seedlings. They have left their plastic flip-flops alongside a raised bank, bright splashes of colour against the dull mud, and donned gumboots. Plastic anachronisms in this primeval land. On the edge of each field is a rough structure, about the size of a door, where the seedlings are grown, a small, plastic-covered hot-house to encourage early germination. Each woman has a wedge of seedlings within easy reach, separated from the whole, floating on the still water. The women have formed a gently curving line, as sinuous as the hardened mud paddy walls that follow the contours of the land and create such pleasing shapes against the dark hillsides throughout this region. Gentle curves trace lines of equal height, still water glints in the sunlight, reflecting the sky, young-green rice seedlings, evenly-spaced, trace random lines in the water. Earth and water and light; stillness broken only by the squelch and suck of a buffalo's plodding feet, the occasional soft command of the driver, the chatter and laughter of the women planting. They wear a mixture of clothing; older women the traditional black pyjamas, loose clothing simply cut; the younger wear what young women wear anywhere in the world: jeans and brightly-coloured blouses. Most have donned conical straw hats, tied under their chins with pieces of cloth, shading their eyes from the sun. They stand calf-deep in mud, bent at the waist, heads down, their hands poking the seedlings deep into the mud with deft prods. They take a small hand full of seedlings from the floating wedge alongside them, hold these in one hand while the other separates a single seedling... prod... separate... prod... separate, backs bent at right angles, gum-booted feet planted deep in the water, they chatter and laugh and plant, moving forward in slow, laborious steps, the line gently undulating as some plant faster than others and leave them behind. They, too, like the man and the water buffalo, have a timeless quality about them, the picture of Middle Age peasants belied by their bright plastic flip-flops and the group of scooters parked just off the roadside, ready to take them home when the day's planting is done.

The road calls to me. I stand and wave; the women see me, stand erect briefly and return my greeting, their laughing cries clear in the still air.

* * * * *

The second time I got wounded was with the LRUPs. We got trapped. Near Duc Pho.

We saw a couple of Viet Congs. We dropped our packs, and chased them. The terrain was so thick there that we lost them. It was jungle. It was the wait-a-minute vines that grab you, tangles you as you move in the jungle. Start gettin' kind of dark, so we go on back to where we dropped our packs.

And that's where they were.

All of a sudden, something said boop. I said I hope this is a rock. It didn't go off. Then three or four more hit. They were poppin' grenades. About ten. One knocked me down. Then I just sprayed the area, and Davis start hittin' with the shotgun. We called for the medivac, and they picked me up. We didn't see if we killed anybody. Only three grenades exploded. The good thing about the Viet Congs was that a lot of their equipment didn't go off.

I told them to give me a local anaesthesia: "I want to watch everything you do on my legs." I don't want them to amputate it. Gung ho shit. But I was OK, and they got the frags out.

From "Bloods" by Wallace Terry

Scooters and a roadside meal

I ride on through farmland and small towns and villages. And the flags - always the flags, red and gold against the green tropical vegetation, attached to roofs and balconies, lifted high above farm houses on tall bamboo poles, tied to the branches of trees. At the roadside, stalls selling garlic and bananas, onions and sugar cane. Bee hives, crudely made and covered with sheets of plastic, cluster in fields. Bullock carts trundle their ponderous way along the road, heavily laden.

Somewhere along this thoroughfare I turn off to follow a small road that climbs into a range of mountains. Once again I am in the forested countryside and my heart lifts with the joy of it. I stop at a roadside shelter where an old woman with arthritic hands serves me boiled eggs and a cob of maize cooked in its skin in a large pot, black with soot, the fire under it filling the air with smoke. When she holds up her hands to show me how much I must pay, her fingers are bent like claws. The woman's hair is grey and she is missing her lower front teeth. In her ears, gold hoop earrings; plastic flip-flops on her feet.

Long lengths of sugar cane with dark purple skins lean against a wall; a rooster, red and glossy black, paces in a wire cage, bobbing his head in frustration, looking for a way out; a cow munches grass on the side of the road. On my low plastic table are bunches of garlic. The air is heavy with the smell of them.

I gnaw on my smoky cob of maize and then start on the boiled eggs. In front of me the rooster bobs his head, sure that if he keeps on looking he will find a way out.

On the road, trucks and the inevitable clutter of scooters pass. Scooters carrying impossible loads - a wheel-barrow, handles leaning against the rider's back; a large wooden wardrobe; a pink pig, trussed up in a metal cage like a sausage, piggy snout protruding from a metal ring at the end of the cage as if sniffing the air; multiple smaller pigs, layered like fish in a tin, trotters and snouts and tails and tits hanging through the bars; windows and large panes of glass; kitchen cupboards; a full-sized fridge.

There are scooters rigged out as shops, fast-food outlets. If the customer won't come to you, you must go to the customer - on a scooter, piled high and wide with displayed produce: pots and pans, vegetables, meat, balloons, plastic goods, cool drinks and crisps. Live fish carried in waterproof canvas tanks, gasping and thrashing about in six inches of water while a small mounted pump, taking its power from the scooter battery, blows bubbles into the water. As I watch, a scooter carrying another scooter, balanced at right angles, comes past, the rider holding it in place with one arm draped carelessly across the seat while he controls his bike with the other hand. Cages full of ducks and chickens, eyes closed, loosened feathers dancing in the wind. Scooters carrying hundreds of kilograms of scrap iron, recycled tins and plastic bottles, logs...

* * * * *

I wish the people in Washington could have walked through a hospital and seen the guys all fucked up. Seventeen-, eighteen-year-olds got casts from head to toes. This old, damn general might walk in and give them a damn Purple Heart. What in the hell do you do with a damn Purple Heart? Dudes got legs shot off and shit, got half their face gone and shit. Anything that you can mention that would make you throw up, that you can possibly dream of, happened.

Can you imagine walking around policing someone's body? Picking them up and putting them in a plastic bag? Maybe you find his arm here, his leg over there. Maybe you have to dig up somebody's grave. Maybe he been there for a couple of days, and it will start stinking and shit. You dig graves. You open graves. You are an animal. You be out there so long that you begin to like to kill. You know, I even started doing that. I walked over a body of a North Vietnamese and said, "That's one motherfucker I don't have to worry about." It made me feel good to see him laying there dead. It made me feel good to see a human life laying down there dead.

From "Bloods" by Wallace Terry

The Delta and Buddhists praying in the street

Some time in the afternoon I miss a turn and before I realise it, I have travelled 50ks in the wrong direction. But I am travelling *through* a country, not pressing on from a to b, so it is of no consequence. In fact, slips like this often are a boon to the traveller because they lead one to the road less taken. My faithful GPS knows the way and leads me along over a hundred picturesque kilometres of small isolated roads through the delta, places I would never had seen had I kept on the main road.

The Red River delta is vast. Even when I am 120ks from the coast, my GPS tells me I am riding at sea level and, at times, somewhat counter intuitively, I am told that I am riding *below* the level of the sea. This whole area is flat, sodden and interwoven with large and small rivers, all nudging their slow way towards the Gulf of Tonkin where they empty their load of sediment into the sea and, as it settles to the ocean floor, the coastline of Vietnam is pushed out by about 100m a year.

Some statistics might be of interest here: The Red River, at 1175ks, is the second longest in Vietnam (the Mekong is much longer at 4350km), its headwaters stretching well into China. Although the delta covers an area of some 15,000 square kilometres, this whole area is less than three metres above sea level, which leads to major flooding during the rainy season when the river increases its flow up to sixty times. Not 60% - 6000%. Normal flow is about 500 million cubic metres a second and, during the floods, water can rise up to fourteen metres above normal levels. Levees have been constructed throughout this region in an attempt to control the floodwaters and protect people's homes and property, but every year major damage and loss of life is caused to the nineteen million people who call this sodden region their home when levees fail and the land is inundated. Despite this danger and the annual disruption of life caused by the floods, deposited silt makes the land extremely fertile and the delta has become one of the leading producers of rice in the world.

It's refreshing to get off the main thoroughfare and into the small tracks again where ordinary people lead their ordinary lives. But I am tiring; the constant vigilance required when negotiating one's way through these impossible roads, the evasive action to avoid sudden death, the constant blasting of horns is wearing me down.

Finally I reach the dual carriageway where I should have been hours before had I not missed my way and am immediately subjected to the inevitable bloody madness, the vehicular mayhem for an hour until I enter the even more chaotic cauldron of humanity that is Ninh Binh.

This dual carriageway has gaps in it every 500m or so to allow cars, trucks, scooters, pedestrians to cross, U-turn, do whatever they like - and they do. Consequently two lanes of traffic (including a large number of diesel-belching behemoths) are barrelling along at a fair lick (well, three lanes, actually, because many of the scooters seek the sanctuary of the hard shoulder) and, into this throng, at regular intervals, a seething mass of vehicles and people attempt to cross at right angles through the gaps in the central reservation. And everyone is hooting. To make matters worse, often you will be confronted by scooters riding the wrong way, keeping mostly to the hard shoulder, of course, but that's where many of the scooters going the *right* way are riding. I come across a man, a pedestrian, who is caught in the middle of this maelstrom, half way across. He stands still, a fixed grimace expressing his state of mind - the wisest thing he can do (stand still, not grimace) - while trucks and buses and scooters blast by on both sides of him. (I imagine coming across a pedestrian standing in the middle of the M6 near Birmingham during rush hour and cannot bear to think of the consequences.)

About five kilometres outside Ninh Binh, I observe something surreal, something one could only expect to encounter in a country like Vietnam: In the fast lane, in the middle of this snarling madness of traffic, a group of about ten Buddhists have laid out their prayer mats, lit candles and are praying. Sorry, but this is so weird it bears repeating: In the *fast* lane of a dual carriageway in the semi-darkness of evening, in the middle of a tangled stream of snarling, raging traffic, a group of men have sat down, made themselves comfortable, lit candles and are praying! And all the drivers simply steer around them. You just need one driver to lose concentration, glance at his mobile phone, drop off to sleep, and they'd all be dead.

That's karma, I suppose.

Having left them behind, for a time I question my sanity. Have I really just seen what I think I've seen?

There are a certain type of people who thrive in cities, speak of the vibrancy of life there, the flashing lights, the pace of life, bars, parties, the press of people, entertainment.

But I hate cities with a passion. They are noisy and impersonal; they lack the human touch; they move too fast. Whenever I enter a city, I find I immediately begin making plans to leave it.

As I write this, I am sitting at a pavement cafe; the hooting of the traffic just a few metres from my face is having an unpleasant effect on my nerves. The voices about me are too loud, the press of people too close. I need to get away into the mountains again. And now a young man serenades us from the sidewalk. He is not content with the natural volume of his voice accompanied by, perhaps, a guitar or mandolin. He drags behind him a portable amplifier and speaker system, attached to a set of wheels. The whole contraption is at least four foot high, and I am assaulted by the sound that pummels me in the face. Local people sitting around me seem not to notice.

Attempting to escape, I take a side road which turns out to be Karaoke Central, flashing lights, gaudy facades, male bouncers and young, female enticers loitering about the streets, inviting casual passers-by to partake of an evening of cultural bliss.

The term quiet sophistication doesn't quite cut it.

I think I am getting old.

* * * * *

The sarge always warned us, "If you want to live, keep off the paths. Don't walk where the fuckin' gooks expect you to walk."

But Mikie, he was new and he was full of shit. Man, he thought he knew it all even though he'd only been in the bush a few weeks. We was setting out and the Sarge says to him, "Mikie, keep off the path -" and he turns to look at the Sarge when a mine explodes under his feet and blows his legs off. He's lyin' there screaming, "Where's my legs, Sarge? Where's my legs?"

I got a piece of shrapnel in my arm and bits of his skin and stuff in my face. And when I'm trying to bandage up what's left of his legs he says to me, "I'm going home, man!" but he died before we got him to the hospital.

The good old British middle-finger salute

After a wake-up shot of coffee, I attempt to make my way out of Ninh Binh and find the road towards Nimh. And immediately I am subjected to the insult, the strident punch in the face of constant and insistent hooting. Despite the calming effect of the coffee, my nerves are soon frayed.

Speaking of coffee, I have to say - although there will be those amongst you who will have differing opinions on this - that if you haven't drunk Vietnamese coffee (or Ethiopian, for that matter), watched it slowly percolate through its little aluminium container on the table in front of you, drop by thick, dark drop, into a small glass tumbler, sweetened condensed milk like a finger-deep, yellow layer of cream at the bottom; then, after lengthy period of reflection and anticipation, waiting for the last drop to detach itself from the bottom of the percolator while the traffic thunders and hoots its way past on the road just metres from your feet, stir it up and pour it into a beer mug filled to the brim with pieces of ice rough cut from a large block, then you have missed something precious in life. Sadly, we in the West have been conned by certain purveyors of a weak, over-priced beverage offered to us using fancy-sounding foreign names so that we assume we're getting something exotic and chic in keeping with the inflated prices they charge. How is it that I can buy a cup of coffee in Vietnam for 30p, the taste of which lingers in my mouth for the next ten miles of riding when in the UK I am asked to pay more than the price of a good pint for something so weak that they suggest I might like to pay even more for a "double shot"?

I believe I'm having a rant. I'm sorry. I could get addicted to this stuff. Drinking it is what I would imagine sniffing a line of Coke must be like. Whooo!

Anyway, I was complaining about the hooting. In South Africa there was a time when mini-bus taxis proliferated and began wreaking their carnage on the roads. As the number of taxis rose, so did the death toll. The cause was multi-faceted: unqualified drivers, over-loading, speeding, ignoring basic traffic rules, un-roadworthy vehicles and the un-sportsmanlike habit of shooting dead rival drivers and their passengers in their frequent turf-wars. Of lesser significance, but still most annoying, was the habit of mini-bus taxi drivers repeatedly toot-tooting their horns as they drove down the street to attract potential customers. As there were hundreds of them in this largely unregulated transport sector, this became more than unpleasant, particularly in the once quiet rural village where we lived.

One afternoon, I rashly allowed my frustration to get the better of my judgement. As one of these toot-tooting taxis came cruising by, I shouted at the driver, waving my arms in a manner that expressed the level of my annoyance. Seeing me react in this unfriendly way, the driver, a large black man, calmly stopped his taxi and got out. It wasn't long before I noticed that he had a pistol in his hand - as one does, in South Africa. Taxi drivers are mostly armed and many have a side-kick who occupies the front passenger seat, also armed, to guard against rival taxi drivers, passengers who might be tempted to steal the day's takings and, sometimes, to shoot unwise traffic policemen in the face who are stupid enough to attempt to impose a fine for a traffic violation.

Or pedestrians who shout at you from the pavement for tooting your horn...

I quickly turned away and acted nonchalant, feeling that it was probably best for my continued health if I made myself scarce and just got used to the hooting.

One would think that, after a while, the brain would accommodate and you'd no longer hear it, like people living next to a railway line who don't hear the trains' passing or those who live under the flight path of Heathrow, but it's difficult to imagine any brain sublimating the strident blare of a truck's horn that is about to run over your back wheel. And it probably wouldn't do your life expectancy much good if it did. But the noise is so loud, so constant, so ever-present on Vietnamese roads that it frays the nerves. I have to confess that there were a few times when I gave the good old British middle finger salute to a few obnoxious drivers - usually in late-model 4X4s with darkened windows - whose manner of hooting was not: Just to let you know I'm here, mate, OK? but was, instead, the mechanical equivalent of: Get out of the **** way or I'll run you over, you ****.

That deserves the finger in my book, whatever country you're driving in. (Although I'm not sure I'd do it in America. They shoot you over there. Or South Africa, if you want to keep on living.)

Finally I reach the sea and make for Cua Lo Beach, supposedly one of the premier resorts in the north of the country. It is, I am sorry to say, a disappointment. An awkward wind blows dust and smoke from burning refuse into the air where it mixes with the smells of salt and decaying fish. The place is run down and dirty.

There are no people here - well, no cute people sunning themselves on white sand, gambolling in clear water against a backdrop of nodding palm trees. It is as depressing as a holiday resort town without holidaymakers can be. Like a fun-fare where there is no fun. The sun is hidden behind an opaque, milky sky. Along the Casuarina-lined beach, rows of empty restaurant booths with their plastic chairs and "Come and Eat" signs in red and yellow stand forlorn. Sad and desperate cries from purveyors of food follow me down the street as they hear the noise of my engine, run outside and gesticulate for my patronage.

At a seemingly desolate and wind-swept car park, I get off my bike to walk out onto the sand and look at the small waves rolling in from a misty sea and am immediately confronted by one of those old crones who seem to frequent places where tourists gather and make life miserable, the old women wearing black shawls who thrust postcards in your face or clutch your clothing begging for alms.

She appears seemingly out of nowhere the moment I have stepped off the bike and is immediately in my face, voice shrill, bad teeth, lottery tickets (I assume) and cards from local hotels clutched in her arthritic fingers.

I try to walk towards the sea but she blocks my way.

I gesture apologetically and say with a grim smile, "No thanks - " but she persists. I say No thanks to her five times then, beginning to lose patience, I ask through gritted teeth, "Please get out of my way."

She holds her ground, voice shrill and insistent.

I repeat, "Please get out of my way," in a flat monotone, restraining in myself an impulse to smack her about the chops. I continue to repeat this about twenty times. It becomes a challenge: I tell myself I will keep repeating Please get out of my way until she backs off.

She doesn't. She wins.

I lose.

I remount my bike and leave, depressed. I hadn't even been able to walk on the beach.

Fortunately, just outside Vinh, I come across some small jetties built into the inlets and mangroves where countless fishing boats, painted in their distinctive red and blue, flags attached to bamboo poles fluttering in the wind, unload their catch. I stop to watch. The fishermen greet me with the plain, disingenuous smiles of the meek, those who will inherit the earth, and I am happy again.

The sturdy wooden construction of these beautiful vessels, the sweeping curves of their hulls so reminiscent of a bird's wing, seem to make them one with the waves and the shoreline; it is as if they have been designed to blend in with the ebb and flow of the tides, the surge of waves - so different from the blunt metal tubs of fishing boats that pound their way through heavy seas around the British Isles and seem alien to their element. I am entranced by these boats, their painted eyes on either side of the prow, the sweet curve of their hulls, the simplicity of design, the red and gold flags that snap and flutter from the superstructure.

Close by, a fisherman and his family eat a meal in the stern of their sampan, their home. Only about 20ft long, it has nets tied in bundles on the prow, their cramped living quarters shielded from the weather by woven strips of bamboo matting. They see me watching and wave a greeting.

Reluctantly, I move on and make my way into the town of Vinh, a dusty, bustling place that was so badly bombed during the American War that it almost ceased to exist. With its proximity to the coast and the maze of small inlets, the muddy, mangrove-sheltered nooks and crannies where small boats can hide and unload cargo, Vinh became the strategic centre for the transfer of food and war materiel from the North onto the Ho Chi Minh Trail where it was secretly carried to soldiers fighting in the South. The Americans were aware of this but - as with so much of the clandestine activity of the Viet Cong - were unable to prevent it. The coastline is a maze of inlets, impossible to police; the North Vietnamese, working only at night in their own back yard, could not be controlled.

The American solution - so often the action of last resort of a powerful nation attempting to subdue a weak but tenacious enemy fighting on home ground - was to bomb the hell out of Vinh from the air, which they did from 1964 until 1972. However the Vietnamese, although technologically handicapped, learned how to shoot down American aircraft and, as the years went by, did so with increasing regularity, often luring them in close and bringing them down with concentrated AK47 fire. In fact, more US aircraft and pilots were shot down over Nghe An and Ha Tinh provinces than over any other part of North Vietnam, which caused the Americans to switch from aerial bombing to shelling the town from battleships anchored off shore.

At the end of the war there were only two buildings left intact in the city. Despite this, delivery of supplies to the South, carried along the Ho Chi Minh Trail, never stopped.

Of course, in the intervening years, Vinh has been rebuilt and there is very little sign of the devastation left after the war. I find a modest hotel and convince the lady receptionist that I will be quite happy with a "basic" room that, after a lot of discussion, she agrees to show me. It's not a room for tourists, she insists, and she's right. But I am happy here. I feel at home. It's somewhat reminiscent of a middle-of-the-road Russian hotel in a backwater Soviet town, but it's an honest room with no pretensions: two beds, a toilet and a shower. What more could you want?

* * * * *

There's this village. No men - just women and children, old people. All huddled up, wonderin' what we gonna do to them. We round them up outside what's left of some huts and I don't know what to do. We already burned up everything - everything, shot all the animals. I think maybe we goin' to take them someplace, put them behind barbed wire, interrogate them. But I don't know so I radio HQ.

A minute later some guy radios back and tells me, "You know what to do, man - waste 'em."

Uncle Ho

If there were saints in Buddhism or if Communism deified its leaders, Ho Chi Minh - or "Uncle Ho" as he is often lovingly referred to - would be a saint of the First Order. Miracles would be claimed at the mention of his name; strands of his hair, toenail clippings, missing fingers and other relics, real or imagined, would be preserved in golden vessels and revered by hollow-eyed supplicants searching for healing and absolution. He is the Vietnamese equivalent to Russia's Lenin, China's Mao Zedong, Cuba's Che, India's Ghandi, Tibet's Dali Lama, South Africa's Nelson Mandela.

His beginnings were humble but, unlike Ghandi, he lacked the pacifist philosophy of life. In fact, his gentle face with its benign smile hid a ruthless and determined mind that would allow nothing to deviate him from his ultimate goal of a united Communist Vietnam free of colonial domination. This extended to sanctioning the slaughter, after the fall of the South, of anyone who might taint the ideal of a pure Communist state. In every town and village it became an orgy of murder, a killing spree of the self-righteous directed towards anyone deemed to be bourgeois: those who owned land or a business, who employed labour, who came from a background of privilege, who were educated - in effect, anyone who was not obviously a member of the downtrodden working class - were methodically and sadistically killed. Lists had been meticulously prepared beforehand and, only hours after the victory, these were dusted off in preparation for the slaughter. Like the Holocaust, it was an attempt to rewrite the history books, to change society not through natural processes, but by eliminating an entire section of the population who had been labelled "deviant".

When the war against the Americans ended and the South imploded, when the inevitable purges began, so many people were rounded up and executed as enemies of the people that Uncle Ho is reported to have said that they "might have been a little too enthusiastic in their purging".

That was nice of him to admit. I'm sure that the families of the murdered received great comfort from his admission.

Maybe that's what the Americans were doing as well, come to think of it...

As the small village of Ho Chi Minh's birthplace, Kim Lien, is only 14ks inland of Vinh and as I have been seeing his benign face smiling at me from a thousand brightly-coloured posters throughout this green and pleasant land, I discard helmet and gloves and, going local, head off to find it.

And I must say I am impressed.

It takes me a while to negotiate my way through the inevitable snarl of traffic until I enter a calm region where there are more rice fields than buildings. A nondescript sign points to the left and, a few minutes off the main road, I am there.

Multicoloured flags; buildings in the Chinese style, beautifully crafted from wood; topiary trees stand in large ceramic pots and smartly uniformed policemen smile a welcome. I park the bike and am given a numbered ticket by a young woman who will look after it for me while I am away for the payment of a few pence. (They write the ticket number in chalk on your seat. It's a good system.)

At the entrance, an official suggests I buy a bouquet of flowers to lay at the altar dedicated to Uncle Ho; I am quite happy to do this small thing as an act of respect but when I reach for my wallet his uniformed colleague bursts out laughing; they wave me through.

An official in uniform with a sense of humour - I am impressed.

I suppose it was inevitable for Ho Chi Minh (born Nguyen Sinh Cung) to become involved in revolution. He grew up in Nghe An province in Central Vietnam, an area that had been at the forefront of resistance to Chinese control of Vietnam which lasted over a thousand years. Then came the French, eager to extend their colonial influence into South East Asia. Opposition to the French was centred here too, with Ho's father one of its leaders. Ho started work as a messenger at the age of nine.

Dismissed from the National Academy in Hue for taking part in protests against the French, Ho worked briefly as a teacher and then as a cook on a steamship. He travelled the world in this way for two years, developing his language skills. In addition to his native Vietnamese, he became fluent in English, Chinese, French, Russian and Thai.

While living in Paris, Ho Chi Minh converted to Communism, travelled to Russia and spent some time in Moscow, eventually living in China close to the border with Vietnam because of the threat of arrest by the French.

During WW2 the Japanese, who also had colonial ambitions in Vietnam, pushed the French out. Ho and others were not prepared to have the hated French removed only for them to be replaced by the Japanese so the Viet Minh was formed, a loose collection of over 10,000 men who began to wage guerrilla war against the Japanese, a skill at which they became particularly adept.

When the Japanese were defeated in 1945, Ho Chi Minh announced the creation of the Democratic Republic of Vietnam. The French, who had not given up their colonial ambitions, refused to recognise the republic. War broke out again. But the French suffered a humiliating defeat at the battle of Dien Bien Phu, a defeat so comprehensive and humiliating that it caused them to pull out of Indo China and not return.

At the Geneva Convention, it was decided to divide Vietnam at the 17th Parallel with North Vietnam governed by Ho Chi Minh and the South by the corrupt Ngo Dinh Diem.

Despite going along with the division of his country, Ho knew that it would only be temporary. He encouraged the Viet Minh resistance movement in the South and ordered that they should be supplied with arms via the trail that was later to be given his name. When the Americans got involved, regular North Vietnamese troops were sent south to assist the Viet Minh and the Vietnam/American War began to spread its bloody net over the entire land.

The North remained stoically loyal to Ho throughout the long war and the continued US bombing raids. In fact, the bombing probably cemented their loyalty as they realised that it was only through this leader that they ever had a chance of being united with the south and completely free of foreign interference.

Hence the museum and the bouquets of flowers laid in front of statues of "Uncle Ho" in an outpouring of veneration and love that is offered to very few long-dead leaders in this world.

Inside the museum, old photographs are displayed: Uncle Ho growing up; a casually dressed Uncle Ho keeping in touch with ordinary people of the soil; after the victory, Uncle Ho meeting with world leaders, visiting factory workers, looking out across newly-built engineering works. In short, Uncle Ho overseeing the emergence of the nascent Communist state. Included, understandably, are paintings and photographs of the past: Vietnamese men and women, their angular bones protruding from beneath starvation-wasted flesh, treated as slave labour by their French colonial rulers. Captions to the photographs could have been lifted from "1984", cluttered with inflated adjectives and purple Communist Speak: "Glorious workers sing happy songs after wondrous victory... "; "Victorious soldiers march with boundless energy after defeating grovelling foe..." (I made those up; can't remember the actual words but many of the captions were couched in that style.)

Strangely, there is very little about the American War and only one reference to the Ho Chi Minh Trail.

One can understand the reverence accorded to this man by most Vietnamese, a man who rose from humble beginnings to the point when he led the nation through an horrific war to the re-unification of north and south after victory against the most powerful nation on earth. Of course it wasn't all smiles and joy for those living in the south who were made to suffer for their part in the war, hence the Boat People exodus so reminiscent of the Syrian Diaspora today.

I leave the museum, the flower-bedecked gilt busts of Ho Chi Minh, the atmosphere akin to that of a holy place, and walk outside into the heat and the bright sunlight. A pathway meanders through manicured gardens and fishponds, past benches beneath shady trees to the unassuming house where Uncle Ho was born. Made from wooden poles, bamboo and palm leaves, he lived here with his mother and father until 1895. The rooms are dark and cool, the floors of beaten earth, window openings shuttered by simple coverings of woven bamboo strips, the doorways so low even the modern Vietnamese have to stoop to move from room to room. A few pieces of furniture grace each room, otherwise it is bare, the house of a peasant.

Outside, a group of schoolchildren listen to a woman telling the story of their great leader and reformer, I assume, and as I walk past I am conscious of my white skin, round eyes and pointed nose that label me foreigner. I want to attract their attention and tell them, I am British, not American, expecting them to look at me with suspicion, call me imperialist dog, war-monger, killer of women and children... but all I receive from them are smiles.

I'm not sure groups of British high school students on an outing would be as well behaved or treat a lone stranger of foreign appearance with such friendly respect.

*****

There was a woman bent over 500 yards away in the fields. She was just harvesting something. We're talking to each other and somebody says, "I'll tell you what. I betcha I can hit her." I said, "Don't be silly. Don't even bother." She was obviously not an enemy agent or anything and she was way out of range.

Everybody started taking pot shots at this woman, just to see if they can hit her. I was the only one that didn't... at first. But something came over me. I was pissed off. I was fucking hot. It was the second day in that fucking tower, you know. I said, "Fuck you guys. Here, watch this." I shot at her and she keeled over dead.

From "Nam" by Mark Baker

Ben Hai River

The next day I continue to ride across a sodden countryside, a land of frogs and ducks and sleek, fat water buffalos. It's their element. And conical-hatted women bent over like question marks, up to their knees in mud, planting seedlings with practiced, methodical proddings. An aqueous land of rivers and estuaries and dams and fish farms and duck ponds and rice-paddies. If the road hadn't been built up as a causeway, it too would be under water.

I ride south on Highway 1 through the rain and the wet, feeling sorry for myself, making. I am making for the Demilitarised Zone, a 5km wide strip on either side of the Ben Hai River that flows east, roughly following the so-called 17th Parallel. The land is flat as a table and wet; it oozes liquid from every pore, resembling a primeval swamp just emerged from the deluge, smelling still of mud and alien things that crawl about, sightless and stinking.

And this is the dry season.

It has drizzled all day so that even the air is wet.

And me.

Biking is great, but biking in the rain, in a foreign land, without the proper protective gear, is not so pleasant. On days like this you just suck it up, put your head down and endure.

And think of home.

The spray-soaked road is straight and boring as it makes its way through dirty towns that have about them that ragged look that small businesses get when they are struggling for survival in an unforgiving market and an uncaring society. I'm quite sure the dull and mizzling weather helps produce this impression, but that's how it seems to me. I feel like the massive truck load of dogs I pass, four levels of wire cages crammed with man's best friends, like those used to carry sheep to slaughter, anxious-looking creatures who seem to know their inevitable fate with the intuition of their breed, dogs who should be chasing sticks in a field or snoring and twitching in front of warm hearths on a winter's night, dreaming of slow cars and fast women.

I suppose they eat dogs here too. I make a mental note to be more careful when I order noodles and "meat" from some nondescript street vendor.

As I ride on, the picture of all those dogs with misery in their eyes stays with me, and another sudden and sobering revelation of the difference in our cultural values comes to mind. There are many ways, I believe, that we are able to assess the social development of a society: the treatment of women; their toleration of free speech and the sharing of ideas; how they treat their animals and, on a more flippant - but no less instructive - note, what facilities are provided for the evacuation of human waste.

I just pray they don't stab, beat and choke the poor dogs to death, skin them alive, like they do in China during the barbaric practice of "softening" the flesh for human consumption.

After three hundred miserable kilometres of wetness and damp, I reach the bridge across the Ben Hai River that marked the border between North and South Vietnam before unification. Even after fifty years, bomb craters, now water-filled, can be seen around the footings of the old bridge.

Ironically, it was here, in the Demilitarised Zone, that some of the heaviest fighting during the American war took place, especially in defending the camps along Highway 9, which roughly follows the river, slightly to the south, established in an attempt to stop infiltration of North Vietnamese soldiers and the carrying of arms and supplies to the Viet Cong fighting in the south. Those carrying materiel south had to cross this road but, despite regular patrols, heavily-defended camps, elaborate hidden listening and movement sensors, nothing the Americans could do stopped the flow.

I leave the river and its iconic metal bridge in the rain and continue 22ks south towards Dong Ha. As I enter the town, a shout from a wizened looking man sitting astride a battered scooter on the side of the road draws my attention. I wave and keep on riding but, moments later, he appears alongside me on his bike, grinning his long, yellow teeth at me, Barbie and Ben plastic helmet wobbling loosely on his head. We conduct the usual shouted conversation whilst negotiating the traffic: Where you from? Where you going?

My hustle detector beeps a warning. He is sizing me up. "You want hotel?" he shouts above the noise of the traffic.

Although I am quite capable of finding a hotel myself, I am tired and wet and it's easier just to nod. He waves for me to follow him and makes a suicidal U-turn across two lanes of heavy traffic. I follow more circumspectly and, within minutes, he leads me into a nondescript hotel.

I use the word "into" intentionally. In most countries, one would use the pronoun "to". But this is not most countries - it's Vietnam. Here one usually drives into a hotel and parks one's bike alongside the reception desk. To be strictly truthful, sometimes there's a separate room to one side where vehicles are kept but often the receptionist is forced to make her way to her desk between ragged lines of scooters. Cars and motorcycles are seldom left on the road. Whether this is just another instance of the tendency of Vietnamese people to extend their living space onto the pavement and, by extension, invite the road and pavement into their living space, or whether endemic vehicle theft has made this practice the norm, I'm not sure.

My diminutive guide quickly dismounts and begins unstrapping my bags. I ask him not to. He grins his yellow teeth at me, still wearing his helmet and cheap blue plastic raincoat and stands back, laughing and addressing the receptionist as if she is a friend. It's obvious that whatever scam they are running, they're doing it together. Nothing wrong with that. Free enterprise and all that. But I am wet, tired and grumpy and don't feel like being hustled. And when a complete stranger smiles his teeth at you and starts untying your bags, you just know you're about to be solicited. He's not doing this for love.

But the hotel is cheap and when he takes out a tatty piece of paper with a sketch map of the DMZ and offers to guide me - on our bikes - to the major battle sites, the tunnels and the North Vietnamese army cemetery, 9am to 3pm for $20 I am already won over. He clutches at my arm in order to press his case more earnestly and I have to detach his fingers. He seems desperate.

I agree to his terms without haggling, even though his rapid and mostly unintelligible Viet-lish will be burdensome on the morrow. His persistence and entrepreneurship deserves some recognition and I'd rather be with him, alone, than part of an organised mini-bus tour. We agree on a time and he disappears.

In my room I spread out all my wet things to dry and ask myself why I do these things when I could be cosy and warm at home.

* * * * *

*L*ike this day, they took this water buffalo from the farmers. Either paid them off or killed them. It didn't matter. Whichever was best.

They lifted it with the Huey about 300 feet. Nobody paid much attention. 'Cause you on a chopper base. You see helicopters liftin' off with all kinds of strange things.

So he flew the chopper up, just outside Bien Hao. The game plan was to drop it. And when you drop a water buffalo 300 feet, it has a tendency to splatter. So that meant the farmers around knew that you were almighty. That you would take their prized possession. That we'll come and get your shit.

So we dropped it in the middle of a minefield. Set off a whole bunch of 'em.

I know the Vietnamese saw it. They watched everything we did.

I think we were the last generation to believe, you know, in the honour of war. There is no honour in war.

My mama still thinks that I did my part for my country, 'cause she's a very patriotic person.

I don't.

From "Bloods" by Wallace Terry

Morning coffee and I become acquainted with Mr Dong

I awake to another miserable day. It is cold and overcast. A sulky rain falls outside my window. Trucks thunder past, hooting, their tyres hissing on the wet road.

I have two hours to kill before my old, behelmeted man is scheduled to arrive to guide me around the battlefields with his earnest clutching of my arm and his unintelligible English. While waiting, I retire to a - what shall I call it? - "cafe" conjures up images of chic tables and lace curtains; "eating house" would be better but there is no food, only coffee. Bare room with plastic tables and infant-sized chairs... Coffee den? Whatever. It is, literally, a bare room open to the street where, between the thundering trucks and us are thirty scooters parked, and completely blocking, the pavement. (Inside, more scooters lean against the sink.) Between the scooters and the road, a pole carrying a festoon of lethal-looking electrical wires stands ready to electrocute the unwary. It does, to give it its due, have a pictorial warning that vaguely resembles a skull with an exclamation mark but it looks more like a wonky Caspir the friendly ghost.

Inside, the bare tile floor is covered with cigarette butts and ash and, as I write, cigarette smoke wafts its noxious fumes over me from the men - they are all men - who sit about smoking, peering into their mobile phones, talking. At one noisy table a group of older men cluster about a board upon which round counters with Chinese characters, red and black, have been arranged; I've seen them before but on a different looking board. The men play with an earnest concentration, slapping the counters down with sharp clicks, exclaiming and groaning according to the success of the move.

The place is run by an old woman and her daughter. The former bustles about in her plastic slip-slops, shouting orders; her daughter washes dishes in the sink next to the parked scooters. On the street outside, a middle-aged man wearing a baseball cap sells bread rolls to customers from a basket woven from bamboo strips. I order coffee. The clear glass with its finger of treacly black liquid in the bottom, an aluminium container filled with coffee on top, hot water slowly dripping through. The sweetened condensed milk at the bottom of the glass forms a clean line between it and the treacle above. A small bowl with a block of ice is deposited on my table but, considering the weather, I'll give that a miss. Water for the coffee is heated on a battered aluminium kettle placed on a thick, cast-iron brazier, like that used for melting precious metals; it is sheltered from the wind outside by a sheet of corrugated iron. On the wall, a TV is showing a children's programme in English - ABC and something about ice cream.

I pay for the coffee - $1.00. Being absorbed, for just these few moments, into the lives of these people is worth far more...

"Vietnam slow-slow, good -" my diminutive guide tells me, laughing. He points at his dilapidated scooter, making a virtue of necessity. His name is Mr Dong, he tells me. "Fast-fast bad," he insists, making sure I understand. I think he means when crossing the road as well as riding on it because we trundle along at just over walking pace through a depressing drizzle that mutes the harsh angles of the cluttered streets.

Then his aged Honda breaks down. We pull off the road. "Twelve year -"

"So I see," I tell him as he crouches over the engine and fiddles. He thinks I'm giving him a compliment.

Finally he coaxes the engine to life and we set off again into the traffic. He leads me to a Vietnamese war cemetery, the white headstones disappearing into the mist. We park our bikes on the roadside and enter through an iron gate, glistening and wet. The cemetery is large, a few acres in size, the grave stones set in neat rows - a telling contrast from the tangled jungle where most of the interned men would have died - man's need for order and uniformity smoothing out the unpleasant wrinkles of history that we prefer not to confront, the horror of the battlefield gentled into neat graves and precisely carved names and flowers, turning mangled victims into heroes.

In front of each grave, bright artificial flowers have been placed; the garish colours jar somewhat with the sombre feel of the place.

"Many people -" he tells me, again stating the obvious but attempting to fulfil his role as guide with the limited number of English words at his disposal.

But he is pointing, not to the neat rows of graves that stretch before us in linear ranks like men standing at attention, but at a number of raised, grass-covered mounds to one side. Only then do I realise that he drawing my attention to a number of ragged, overgrown mass graves which evidently hold the body parts of multiple victims ripped into unidentifiable bits in the many bombing raids that devastated this place.

Carved into almost all of the grave stones is the same phrase. I ask what it says.

"Martyr," Mr Dong translates, bringing his hands together, palms down, overlapping, then spreading them wide. "No name."

He explains, and I manage to understand, that American soldiers wore aluminium dog tags and, because of this, their bodies could be identified even if found years later when everything else had rotted away. Vietnamese soldiers had no such means of identification but some used to write their names on pieces of rice paper, sealed in small bottles to keep them dry and kept in their pockets. But often the bottles were shattered along with the bodies that held them and the rice paper would quickly disintegrate in the wetness of the climate, so many bodies remain unidentified. As most of the North Vietnamese and Viet Cong were fighting very far away from their homes and communication was, at best, primitive, families could be left for years not knowing that a son or husband had been killed. Usually they had to wait until someone who had survived a battle and who had witnessed the death came home and could tell them in person what they had seen.

Missing in action... A dreadful phrase with all the heartache and lack of closure it implies. The 2265 American m.i.a. have exercised the conscience of the nation since the end of the war but little mention is ever made of the 300,000 Vietnamese soldiers who are still missing, their lost bodies long since rotted away into the wet jungle soil.

The Americans developed a sophisticated system of getting their dead and wounded out of a battle zone using helicopters so that most wounded would be picked up and removed to a hospital or treatment centre within hours; Vietnamese wounded had to get out on their own, usually on foot, sometimes with the limited help that any of their friends could offer. There were a few basic hospitals hidden in the forest or in underground tunnels where the wounded could be treated but these were rudimentary at best, often using medicine stolen from the Americans, taken off dead bodies or scavenged from downed aircraft. These treatment centres - it would give a false impression to call them hospitals, although complex operations were undertaken there - had to be hidden and were often moved at short notice because American troops would destroy them and kill all personnel whom they classified as the enemy or, at best, "assisting the enemy".

During the war, a moving diary was discovered by an American, Fred Whitehurst, who was serving with a military intelligence detachment at Duc Pho base. It was his job to sift through thousands of captured documents and destroy those with no military value. One day, while throwing waste into a 55-gal drum to be burned, he came across a collection of pages sewn together with a cardboard cover. He decided to keep it. Later he asked a Vietnamese friend to read out passages to him and translate them. It turned out to be Vol. 2 of the diary of a 25-year-old, newly-qualified doctor, Dang Thuy Tram, who, despite her youth, travelled south along the Ho Chi Minh Trail, tasked with setting up a clinic in the bush to treat wounded North Vietnamese soldiers.

"Human to human," Whitehouse said, "I fell in love with her."

After serving three tours in Vietnam, he took the diary home with him and, years later, managed to trace Thuy Tram's mother and return the diary to her. It was eventually published as *Last Night I Dreamed of Peace* and has been translated into many languages. The diary shows with poignant tenderness a view of the war, of the enemy, from the "other" side, giving the North Vietnamese and Viet Cong a human face that has been lost in the many USA-centric interpretations of the war. Inside this book we read the achingly honest words of a young woman, desperately unsure of herself and the immense responsibilities she is required to bear, earnestly seeking acceptance into the Communist Party, hopelessly in love with a young man involved in the fighting in another place.

I include here some excerpts from Dang Thuy Tram's diary because they, more than anything I can write, will give the lie to the common impression that all Vietnamese were nameless, faceless and expendable:

22 April 1968

Oh, Huong! Huong died! The news stuns me like a nightmare. One comrade falls down today, another tomorrow. Will these pains never end? Heaps of flesh and bones keep piling up into a mountain of hatred rising ever taller in our hearts. When? When and when, comrades? When can we chase the entire bloodthirsty mob from our motherland?

1 November 1968
Yesterday, there was a twenty-one-year-old man with wounds all over his body. He called my name as though I could save him, but all I could do was weep as I watched him die in my powerless hands.

I see it now: in the South, the flowers of victory and heroism are blooms of flesh and bones, of many young lives. I am walking in the centre of the South in the middle of that flower garden, my heart filling with so much admiration, pride, and immense pain when each flower falls. I have always loved flowers, but now with each step, my appreciation for the true beauty of flowers has given me a deeper understanding of love, hate and pride.(You're also a beautiful flower, aren't you, my little brother?)

8 November 1968

Sitting next to you, my young brother, holding your warm hands, I am in anguish because there is no way for me to protect you. If you fall in this atrocious struggle... oh, my young brother! I will remember forever this moment, remember all my life your bright, affectionate eyes, your tender words. Oh, young brother, I am afraid. If you die, when will my pain subside? Each time you confess your love to me, I am shaken by a strange emotion.

Why can we, revolutionists, love each other so much? A love as deep and immense as the ocean, a love that surges like frothing waves, passionate, pure.

26 February, 1969

A spring night, the moon is strangely clear. I want to put away the intense feelings in my heart and focus on work, but it's impossible. I don't know what can possibly drain my heart of longings, dreams and hopes. Last year, even in an underground chamber, hearing the sounds of the enemy searching for us above, I still told them Khiem Pavel's story. In the middle of the enemy's operation, bombs and bullets fell around me as I sat inside a crack in the mountain and wrote my letters and diary. Now, beneath this mountain of work, I am still a person with a soul burning for life.

13 March 1969

Another comrade sacrificed his life. The wound went all the way through his abdomen. His condition was not good after the operation, and worsened over time. Perhaps there was an internal haemorrhage caused by some undiscovered shrapnel cutting a vein. After a joint diagnosis, the common opinion was not to perform a second operation. Privately, I hesitated. In the end he died. I developed a severe headache, thinking about his death. Why did he die? Was it because of my indecision? Very probably. If I had been decisive, he might have had a ten percent chance of survival. I conformed to the majority's opinion and dropped something worth doing.

He died with a small notebook in his breast pocket. It held many pictures of a girl with a lovely smile and a letter assuring him of her steely resolution to wait for his return. On his chest, there was a little handkerchief with the embroidered words: Waiting for you.

Oh, that girl waiting for him! Your lover will never come back; the mourning veil on your young head will be heavy with pain. It will mark the crimes committed by the imperialist killers and my regret, the regret of a physician who could not save him when there was a chance.

I don't know what people think when they see the American bandits' air raids. This afternoon, like other afternoons, an OV-10 plane circles several times above the hamlets, then launches a rocket down onto Hamlet 13 in Pho An. Immediately, two jets take turn diving down. Where each bomb strikes, fire and smoke flare up; the napalm bomb flashes, then explodes in a red ball of fire, leaving dark, thick smoke that climbs into the sky. Still, the airplanes scream overhead, a series of bombs raining down with each pass, the explosions deafening.

From a position nearby, I sit with silent fury in my heart. Who is burned in that fire and smoke? In those heaven-shaking explosions, whose bodies are annihilated in the bomb craters? The old lady sitting by me stares at the hamlet and says, "That's where Hung's mother-in-law lives."

29 July 1969

The war is extremely cruel. This morning, they bring me a wounded soldier. A phosphorus bomb has burned his entire body. An hour after being hit, he is still burning, smoke rising from his body. This is Khanh, a twenty-year-old man, the son of a sister cadre in the hamlet where I'm staying. An unfortunate accident caused the bomb to explode and severely burned the man. Nobody recognises him as the cheerful, handsome man he once was. Today his smiling, joyful black eyes have been reduced to two little holes - the yellowish eyelids are cooked. The reeking burn of phosphorus smoke still rises from his body. He looks as if he has been roasted in an oven.

His mother weeps. Her trembling hands touch her son's body; pieces of his skin fall off, curled up like crumbling sheets of rice cracker. His younger sisters are attending him, their eyes full of tears.

A girl sits by his side, her gentle eyes glassy with worry. Clumps of hair wet with sweat cling to her cheeks, reddened by exhaustion and sorrow. Tu is Khanh's lover. She carried Khanh here. Hearing that he needed serum for a transfusion, Tu crossed the river to buy it. The river was rising and Tu didn't know how to swim, but she braved the crossing. Love gave her strength.

The pain is imprinted on the innocent forehead of that beautiful girl. Looking at her, I want to write a poem about the crimes of war, the crimes that have strangled to death millions of people, but I cannot write it.

2 June 1970
Nearly a whole night without sleep, we go at first light. Leaving again. The resistance against the Americans to save the country may last longer, our countrymen may have to sacrifice more property and lives, but we will surely win...

Oh, Uncle Ho, your words still reverberate in my ears, and at this moment they mask the sound of bombs and bullets, they are in my heart everywhere I go.

And then, shortly before the war's end, she is killed.

It happened like this (I quote from the last paragraph of the book):

On the morning of June 22, 1970, soldiers from a company of the Americal Division (D Company of the 4th Battalion, 21st Infantry) heard the sound of "a radio playing VN music and voices of people talking" while out on patrol. Later that day, the 2nd Platoon spotted four people moving towards them down a jungle trail. One of them was Dr Dang Thuy Tram, dressed in black pants and a black blouse, and wearing Ho Chi Minh sandals. The Americans opened fire, killing Thuy and a young NVA soldier named Boi.

"The other two evaded off the trail and were lost by the element," according to the after-action report.

Discovered among Thuy's possessions were a Sony radio, a rice ledger, a medical notebook with drawings of the wounds she treated, bottles of Novocain, bandages, poems written to an NVA captain along with his photograph - and this diary.

The bridge

Mr Dong's voice pulls me back to reality.

He sweeps his hand over the massed graves and says one word, "Hero." Then, with chopping movements aimed at his arm and legs he adds, "Dead -" and a disturbing image of dismembered bodies enters my mind. "Me -" he continues, pointing to himself and miming a gun firing and himself running away. Then he smiles: "One year..."

"Me too," I assure him, acknowledging that I too would probably want to run away if confronted by heavily-armed soldiers intent on killing me or aircraft dropping canisters of Napalm that will melt my flesh.

He explains that he was fourteen when the war came to his village. The fighting continued all around the area in which he was living until he turned eighteen and he was called up. He served one year in the NVA - the North Vietnamese Army - until the war ended.

There is a special irony about this war cemetery. Whether intentional or not - I couldn't make myself sufficiently understood - but Dong tells me that it has been built right on top of the site of a major American base during the war.

We cross the road in the rain, careful not to get killed. Dong assures me there is the wreck of an American tank in the undergrowth close by. We make our way along a muddy path through grass and weeds beaded with raindrops. Partly hidden by overgrown bushes is the rusted hulk of a tank. We clamber up and stand on the hull; the turret and gun have been blown off and lie half hidden in a tangle of weeds. I wonder why more has not been made of it, why it has been left here slowly disappearing into the undergrowth.

We take our lives in our hands and cross the road again, mount the bikes and make our way to the bridge across the Ben Hai River, 22ks north of Dong Ha. Alongside the new bridge is the old, a riveted metal girder structure painted blue on the northern side and yellow on the south. The bridge is now preserved as a memorial, a rusted metal reminder of the physical and ideological separation of the two halves of this long, narrow country. It is not the original. That was, logically, painted red on the northern half and yellow on the south and was bombed by the Americans in 1967. The present, old bridge was re-built in 1973 after the signing of the Paris cease-fire agreement - a tactical ploy which both the Americans and Ho Chi Minh were determined to ignore. A high flagpole bears aloft a huge Vietnamese flag on the northern bank, a triumphal statement. The rusting bridge is falling apart now and vehicles are prohibited from using it; the wooden slats that make the roadway are rotten and expose the river far below.

On the southern bank is a memorial, an angular statue of a woman and child, gazing across the river surrounded by six tall feather-like steles. It has been erected to commemorate all the women and children who were left behind when their husband-fathers went off to fight and who waited, often for years, for news about whether they were still alive. Many were never heard of again - approximately 300,000 Vietnamese m.i.a. whose bodies have never been found.

Dong points to another statue on the northern bank and tells me it is in memory of a young woman who lived near here and who relayed information to the North Vietnamese forces by radio about American troop movements until she was killed by a bomb.

Outside the museum are displayed two large speakers, sieved with bullet holes, which were used to amplify propaganda to the enemy on the southern bank of the river. Inside the museum are displayed the leftover detritus of war as well as photographs of children maimed by unexploded ordinance abandoned throughout this region and, in fact, all over Vietnam, after the war. Other photographs show American soldiers running helter-skelter towards their helicopters, pursued by valiant North Vietnamese soldiers; of captured American airmen being guarded by peasants armed with little more than sickles and hoes; joyous citizens from north and south re-united after the war as if the only impediment to mutual love and understanding was the hated American invader. Other photographs show peasants ploughing over the bomb craters, smoothing the ugly face of war and replacing it with green fields of rice after the war had ended.

And, of course, photographs of Ho Chi Minh...

Seeing me looking at a picture of his beloved Uncle Ho, Dong stands at my side and says, "No family... us children -" pointing at his chest where his heart lies. "Fighting... freedom..." and these words are enough for me to understand.

* * * * *

I was just telling them, "I want you to keep your heads down. Keep your eyes open. We got snipers up here."

Stanley responded like I was telling him. Donald took his time and was laughing. They were sitting behind a little knoll. Donald sits up facing the outside of the perimeter. As I was telling him to keep his eyes open, all of a sudden there's this pow!

The bullet went through Donald's upper shoulder, came out his chest and went through Stanley's arm. Stanley panicked.

When it hits the kid, he didn't die right away. He looked at me and all I could see were the tears in his eyes. It was like he was saying, "I'm alive, but what do I do? I'm dying."

I debated whether I should put a bullet in his head and take him out of his misery. For some reason I couldn't do it. I looked at him, he was a young kid. He was seventeen when his parents signed for him to get in the service.

From "Nam" by Mark Baker

Vinh Moc Tunnels

We ride in the rain to the beach and stop at a cafe-restaurant built on wooden piles over lumpy swells that sweep up the beach under the wooden floorboards before sucking back. The scene has a wildness about it accentuated by the heavily overcast sky and a nasty wind that blows the tall palms about with a dry rustling of fronds.

I stare out at the sea while Dong negotiates with a small woman who lifts fish of various sizes out of the fridge until one is decided upon. Under cover from the rain and lazing about on the plastic chairs are a group of men already word-slurring drunk and four girls in their late teens. Dong summonses one and insists that she drapes her arms around my neck for a photograph and I reluctantly allow it to happen. It has too much of the corny Facebook moment about it - like tourists posing on camels in the desert for no other reason than to lay claim to the fact that they've been there.

There is a forced quality to the young woman's laughter and an emptiness in her eyes that I cannot place as we mechanically go through the motions. In my naivete, I don't at first associate these attractive, chattering girls with the oldest profession but a short while later, while Dong and I are tucking into our fish and noodles, one of the inebriated men gets loosely to his feet and takes a girl by the arm. They make their slow, tottering way up some wooden stairs, she giggling and glancing back at her friends while he concentrates on not falling over, to a room on the first floor.

And I am deeply saddened, angry at Dong for using the girl as a photographic prop, for manipulating me into playing a part I want nothing of.

A short while later two men in their thirties ride up on a loaded motorcycle. One is Vietnamese who speaks good English; the other, I discover, German. He sits at an empty table while his guide orders a meal. I engage the young man in conversation and he tells me he is touring Vietnam on a bike and has employed this man, who runs a tour company, to act as his driver, guide, interpreter and general factotum.

Whilst it is good that a person of more timid nature should still experience something of the joys of travel, I look at him and reflect that we are creatures apart. If I were offered the opportunity of riding pillion behind someone whose task it was to ride the bike and guide me around a foreign country for *free*, I would refuse.

What would be the point?

While the German sat in his own bubble of solitude, his guide was sorting out his meal, chatting to the girls, organising his life. He had, in a way, placed the man as a barrier between himself and the local Vietnamese people.

The whole joy of travel, surely, is in the struggle to find your own way, getting lost and discovering yourself in out-of-the-way places, sleeping in dodgy hotels, attempting to communicate without the blessing of a shared language, interacting with local people. It's much easier if someone else does it all for you, of course, but I believe one would emerge from the experience having missed out on something special, without having dug ones toes into the dust of the land, shared the smell of it and the idiosyncrasies of its people at first hand.

Each to his own, I suppose.

Fishy meal eaten, we leave the girls and the young German man behind and, after a short ride along small roads, come to the tunnels.

Steps cut into the firm clay, muddy from the rain, descend steeply into the earth. All about on the surface are craters, now overgrown with vegetation, that bear testimony to the heavy bombing from the air and shelling from the sea that this area suffered as the Americans attempted to destroy the tunnels which they knew were there.

But nothing could dislodge those who were living deep down inside them. As Dong and I make our way deeper and ever deeper under the earth, the passage becomes lower and more narrow, claustrophobic. I run my fingers along the sides; the clay is firm and smoothly cut, ideal for burrowing into and holding its form. Dark passages branch off periodically and still we descend, the air warm and thick with moisture.

Eventually the tunnel levels off. It is too low for me to stand upright in, although Dong has no problem. The sides seem to press in on me as I follow his silhouetted figure, lit by the dim glow of a torch. At intervals, small cells have been hollowed out on either side - rooms for families to live and sleep in, Dong informs me, although they cannot be much larger than a double bed.

The genesis of the Vin Moc tunnels is, I believe, of interest. In 1966, the Americans started a concentrated aerial and artillery bombing of North Vietnam. The people of Vinh Moc village found themselves living in one of the most heavily bombed and shelled pieces of land on earth. Although by this time all families had their own bomb shelters dug close to their homes, these were not deep enough to withstand this onslaught; villagers either fled or began tunnelling deeper into the red-clay earth.

Seeing the potential of this, the Viet Cong encouraged the villagers to stay, using their tunnels as a base for their counter insurgency operations. Excavated earth was carefully camouflaged to prevent its detection from the air and after over a year of work, an enormous VC base had been established underground. Villagers by this time had given up living on the surface and had made their homes in the tunnels where they remained for the duration of the war despite incredible hardship. Seventeen babies were born in the underground delivery room during this time.

Later, the civilians and VC were joined by North Vietnamese soldiers whose mission was to keep communications and supply lines to the south open.

Other surrounding villages also built tunnel systems, but none were as deep or elaborate as Vinh Moc. The poorly constructed tunnels of Vinh Quang village (at the mouth of the Ben Hai River) collapsed after repeated bombing, killing everyone inside.

The tunnels went as deep as 26m below the ground with some entrances on the high bluff overlooking the sea while others opened right onto the beach. Heavily camouflaged, these entrances made it easy to transfer war materiel brought across by boat from bases on Con Co Island to be moved on to North Vietnamese soldiers fighting in the south using the network of the Ho Chi Minh Trail.

The only bomb able to penetrate to the lower tunnels was the dreaded "drilling bomb" that was able to penetrate deep into the earth before detonating. Only once did one of these bombs score a direct hit but it failed to explode. No one was injured and the inhabitants adapted the bomb hole for use as an airshaft.

On our way home, Dong stops at a fish market on the edge of a calm inlet where blue and red painted fishing boats, their heavy planking curved sweet as birds' wings, bob in the rising tide.

"Qu go' fish ling-ling?" Dong asks me in his heavily accented Viet-lish, pointing.

My brain takes a few seconds to translate but, having spent the day with him, my ear is attuned to his accent and vocabulary. "Yes," I assure him, "we do indeed have fish in England."

Women crouch in front of their small piles of fish, resting back on their feet, knees spread wide beneath their skirts, balanced in a way impossible for us Westerners used all our lives to sitting on chairs. They greet me with sweet smiles, call me over to look at their fish even though they know I will not buy.

Dong buys a large fish that, he tells me, he will take home for his family's evening meal. He tucks it into a plastic bag hanging from the handlebars into the foot-well of his bike. We mount and head back into Dong Ha, stopping on the way at a museum where, outside, is displayed a large US tank, Chinese 6X6 trucks and a Sam 6 missile, supplied by the Russians, that changed the nature of the air war. Before the Sam 6, Vietnamese soldiers had to rely on their AK47s to bring down enemy aircraft. Unlikely as this was, they had successes by using cunning, especially after an aircraft had crashed. Knowing that the Americans would immediately send rescue craft in an attempt to extract any crew left alive, the VC would set a trap by lighting a fire in the vicinity of the crash. Rescue aircraft, looking for signs of life, would come in low to investigate the smoke or, if at night, the light cast by the fire. As soon as the aircraft was close enough, every North Vietnamese soldier would fire his AK47, creating what became known as a "Christmas tree" of tracer, the aircraft like the star at the top. This concentrated fire would often be sufficient to bring another aircraft down.

But the Sam 6 changed all this. It was so fast and powerful and had such a high ceiling that even high-flying B52 bombers, that previously had been impervious to the crude anti-aircraft fire available to the North Vietnamese, could be shot down.

Back at the hotel, I pay Mr Dong the fee we agreed on. There was nothing he had shown me, really, that I couldn't have found on my own, but his gentle, smiling presence, his quaint way of speaking, the fact that he had been here as a young lad while the fighting was going on in his own back yard, made the day special.

* * * * *

We were riding in a jeep, about five of us. The driver said jokingly, "Will anybody bet me that I won't hit that old woman walking along the side of the road?" There was an old woman walking along with a long pole over her shoulder, a big bag of rice on each end.

"Yeah, I dare you," one of the guys said. He just turned the wheel real quick and broke her damn hip.

That was the worst thing I saw over there. I didn't see any massacres. It was a guy on a dare. He wasn't a psycho, he wasn't a nut. For some reason something compelled him to run that old lady down.

From "Nam" by Mark Baker

Sampans and a rat the size of a rabbit

Later it is evening and the rain has stopped. Even the air feels clean. I head out of town on foot to explore the riverbank. Moored alongside a concrete jetty, badly undermined and tilting, grey-painted Coastal Patrol vessels rust quietly in the muddy water. No one is about. There is a tiredness about them that testifies to months of inaction. Clothing hangs on a piece of rope tied between the mast and a railing stanchion.

Further out in the river, sampans *put-put* through turgid, slow-flowing water. I walk along the riverbank. Weeds come up to my waist, tangle my boots. Under the road bridge, five sampans are moored up for the night. It is clear that each small boat is home to a family and I struggle to comprehend how even a single person can live in so constricted a place, but throughout this country extended families do. Clothing hangs from pieces of rope tied between poles; a woman crouches in the stern of one sampan and washes dishes, scooping river water into a plastic bowl. Small children notice me watching and wave, their heads poking through the woven bamboo matting that serves for a curved roof over where they live and sleep and eat, rocked by the dirty brown water flowing past them on its way to the sea.

I long to visit them in their narrow boat-homes so that I can better understand lives lived so differently from my own, but they are moored quite far out and there are no boats to carry me there. I wave again, hoping that perhaps someone will ferry me across.

No one comes.

The woman washing dishes stands, flings the water back into the river and smiles at me.

Under the bridge it is almost dark now. A silhouetted sampan makes its way through the water, the owner standing in the stern to control the long, extended propeller shaft, keeping its flailing blades just below the surface. The vegetation on the bank softens, blends into the darkness. The river becomes a mirror and everything is still.

As I turn away I can hear soft voices from the moored sampans and moving shadows behind the woven matting.

Feeling that even my watching is an intrusion, I make my way up the bridge bank and into the seething morass of the town. As with all emerging economies, I find myself making my way through the meeting place of two worlds: the old and the new; the very poor and the rich; those forging ahead as Vietnam opens up to the rest of the world and, mostly the old, those being left behind, still clinging to a lifestyle that has already passed - they just haven't noticed its passing. So, a brightly-lit shop filled with electrical goods, mobile phones, gleaming motor scooters - a large emporium that would co-exist without incongruity in any modern twenty-first century city - rubs shoulders with a one-roomed hardware store, the owner sitting, disconsolate in the gathering dark, as dusty and immobile as his wares; outside a chic restaurant, an old crone crouches in front of a brazier, aluminium pot of noodles steaming in the heat, smoke-blackened teapot and glasses set out on a tray. She attracts no customers and I wonder how long she will crouch there on the pavement before she packs up in the dark and makes her solitary way home. A brightly-lit supermarket stands next to an old canvass-covered market, dingy and smelling of rotting vegetables. I pass a karaoke bar outside of which a peasant woman wearing a conical hat crouches alongside her basket of farm produce, a flickering hurricane lantern her only illumination. From somewhere joss sticks fill the air with their sweet, pungent odour. A rat, as large as a rabbit, scuttles past an elegant shop front. He is no respecter of persons. A little further on two smaller rats - but still larger than my extended hand - tumble in the gutter, mating, fighting, who knows.

A thin young man approaches me and asks for money. My first beggar in Vietnam. I reach for my wallet. He comes up close, puts both arms around me and hugs me. And I smell the booze on his breath. For obvious reasons I usually don't give money to those whose lives are indebted to alcohol but, by reaching for my wallet, I have committed myself and his hug has already given me thanks so I take out a small note and place it in his hand.

He is not impressed and asks for more...

I walk away. Our interaction has been a disappointment for both of us.

Bored with street food, I buy myself fruit for my supper.

* * * * *

In Vietnam and in Lorton I was with men at their darkest hour. We listened to Aretha Franklin together in both places. And we cried together, and longed for the World together.

War is prison too.

About a year ago I saw Streeter on a D.C. transit bus. He was having problems. He would express that he could not find a job. He had lost his wife. He was talking very slow and very deliberate. His speech had slowed down. His whole demeanour had slowed down.

I think that what happened to him in Vietnam was the damagingest thing I seen happen to one person.

I did not know how he felt about me seeing him again back in the World.

I did not know what to say to him.

From "Bloods" by Wallace Terry

Body count

I am up early, ready for the long haul down the Ho Chi Minh Trail, Highway 14, and find that it is still raining. Procrastinating, I walk up the rain-wet pavement to look for coffee.

Later, even though it is still raining, I load up the bike. Soon I am out of the urban sprawl and into the mist and greenery of the mountains. By mid-morning, the rain hides its drippy face although the sky is still heavily overcast. I pass a man on his scooter - a true entrepreneur - who has fitted a wood-burning stove onto the back of his bike, spare stock of wood to keep the fire going, large pot bubbling away over the fire, ingredients and stuff packed into a cabinet fitted to the other side and a loudspeaker connected to the bike's battery advertising his wares. He rides along in front of me, smoke billowing out the back of the bike from the fire, steam seeping from beneath the lid of the pot, loudspeaker blaring...

I'm not sure Health and Safety plays a significant part in the lives of people over here.

Highway 9. Originally constructed by the French in the early 20th century, this road - the term "highway" is a misnomer - traverses the country at its narrowest point from the sea, through Dong Ha to the border with Laos in the west. Its significance lies in the fact that it roughly follows the path of the Ben Hai River that, from 1954 to 1975 marked the division between the Republic of Vietnam (South Vietnam) and the Democratic Republic of Vietnam (North Vietnam).

But the division of Vietnam into North and South began much earlier. At the Potsdam Conference held in Berlin two months before the end of WW2, America, Great Britain and Russia decided that the occupying Japanese forces in the south would surrender to the British while those in the north would surrender to the Chinese. The concept of a divided Vietnam was thus entrenched; furthermore, the seeds of a Communist leaning north were sown while the south remained within the sphere of Western hegemony. Nearly a decade later, in April 1954, Geneva, Ho Chi Minh's government agreed to a cessation of hostilities and the creation of a Demilitarised Zone situated along the route of the Ben Hai. The peace deal stipulated that a 5km strip north and south of the river would be demilitarised by both sides and that, more importantly, it would only be temporary and would not constitute a political boundary. Ho Chi Minh was still determined to continue the fight for a united Vietnam and the French, realising that they were steadily losing their attempt to raise their flag permanently in this part of Indochina, were desperate for a reprieve. The move was merely tactical for both sides, signatures on a piece of paper that gave everyone breathing space before the inevitable conflict was renewed.

Which, of course, it did. The French were eventually so badly beaten and demoralised at the battle of Dien Bien Phu that they gave up their colonial ambitions in this part of the world and pulled out, never to return.

This left the Americans.

And, during the American/Vietnam War, this so-called Demilitarised Zone became the scene of some of the bloodiest fighting of the war as the North Vietnamese soldiers infiltrated to the south and the Americans attempted to stop them, setting up defensive camps along Highway 9: Cua Viet, Gio Linh,

Dong Ha, Con Thien, Cam Lo, Camp Carroll, The Rockpile, Ca Lu, Khe Sanh and Lang Vay.

As I ride in the drizzle up Highway 9, I look out for evidence of the camps, hoping to explore them, to stand in the place where such bitter and bloody fighting took place, but, as it does, nature has almost completed its cleansing process, wiping away the atrocities of man by a gentle greening. I can find nothing, although I know that traces are still there. Certainly many unexploded bombs and shells remain as thousands of Vietnamese have been killed and maimed by the ordinance left after the fighting ended.

At Dakrong Bridge I ignore the junction that leads onto Highway 14, the Ho Chi Minh Trail, and take the small road that leads to what is left of the Khe Sanh Combat Base. The road climbs through wooded hills onto a plateau upon which the small town of Khe Sanh has been built. I ask and get directions. The air is misty and wet as I stand on what is left of the air field, overgrown now and surrounded by stilted wooden homes and small plots of vegetables: I try but fail to re-enact in my mind one of the most bloody sieges of the American War, lasting seventy-five days and costing the lives of over 500 American and 10,000 North Vietnamese troops and hundreds of local people who got caught up in the cross-fire.

Briefly, what happened was this: The Khe Sanh base was initially established by the Americans to recruit and train local hill people so that they could be used against the North Vietnamese. Later it was enlarged and manned by US Army Special Forces as a stronghold in the area. In a prelude to the initially very successful Tet offensive a short while later, the North Vietnamese massed troops in the hills surrounding the base and began advancing towards it. The Americans became aware of this and began flying in reinforcements and equipment to defend the base. President Johnson was worried that he was about to be faced with an American version of the Dien Bien Phu battle that demoralised the French and he was determined, at any cost, not to give ground. The North Vietnamese were equally determined and what resulted was a protracted and bloody siege. The Americans had over 5000 aircraft for attack and support and, during the siege, they dropped 100,000 tons of explosives on the attacking North Vietnamese troops.

In the end, the firepower and technological superiority of the US forces enabled them to prevent the base from being overrun. But, as so often happened in this senseless war, a mere three months later the base was deemed "no longer necessary". The Americans removed whatever was portable and blew up what was not... and left.

Trying to understand the futility of this war, to imagine what it must have been like fighting here in these densely wooded hills, shrouded in mist, beautiful now in their peaceful solitude, I mount my bike and ride back to Dakrong Bridge and then take the turn onto the main Ho Chi Minh Trail, heading for Aluoi, 65ks to the south. Aluoi was an important US Special Forces base until it was overrun and abandoned in 1966, after which it became an important North Vietnamese staging post for supplies moving down the trail. As I ride, I am aware that somewhere to my left, hidden in millions of acres of mountainous forest, is Hill 1175, Hill 521 just inside the Laotian border and, further south, Hamburger Hill.

To claim that I've been riding the HCMT all day is disingenuous but it sounds good. The road - Highway 14 - is marked at the beginning by a large concrete plaque which informs one that this is, indeed, the Trail, but there is clearly no relation between this well-constructed tar road and the network of small tracks through the hills and forest that countless North Vietnamese soldiers traversed with their impossibly heavy loads during the war. Trucks came later as the marked tracks were widened and developed into rudimentary roads, carefully concealed under the dense tropical canopy overhead. Whenever the US pilots managed to discover a section of the trail it was heavily bombed but a way round was quickly constructed, a new route found, and the supplies kept heading south. And so what is thought of by many as a single "trail" became a network, like the meandering tributaries of a river that make their way across a wide flood plain: block one tributary and the water will simply find another way.

At that time, traversing the Ho Chi Minh Trail was so stressful and dangerous that many thousands of North Vietnamese cadres never made it to the end. And it wasn't only the Americans they had to contend with: more dangerous and debilitating was malnutrition and disease - mostly malaria - which took its toll. Each soldier on the trail was supplied with a small bag of rice but this was soon exhausted. At the rest camps set up in the forest, at intervals of roughly one day's march, there sometimes was food but often, after an exhausting day carrying a heavy load or pushing a laden bicycle along roughly-cut tracks through the forested mountains in whatever weather the highlands of Central Vietnam could fling at them, soldiers had to forage themselves for whatever food they could garner from the jungle. Often they went hungry. Increasingly vigilant American patrols disrupted re-supply, killing anyone they thought might be assisting the enemy, and forcing the exhausted, ill and starving soldiers to keep moving, living lives of hunted animals.

Those who fell ill would be left behind by their comrades to recover, or not, over time. When sufficiently well recovered, the soldiers would pick up their loads and continue along the trail.

In a few places temporary first aid stations were established but these were constantly harassed by American forces who would destroy them and kill all they found there - soldiers, wounded as well as doctors and nurses - regarded as "legitimate" targets. Nurses and, occasionally, a doctor who ran these aid stations had to grow or acquire their own food because very often supplies of rice to feed the wounded and ill soldiers and nurses couldn't get through.

Life became significantly more difficult for those using the trail after the US began using Agent Orange - a mixture of equal parts of two herbicides, 2,4,5-T and 2,4-D - given its name from the orange-striped barrels in which it was shipped. This was contaminated with the extremely toxic 2,3,7,8-Tetrachorodibenzodioxin. Concentrations in soil and water after spraying with Agent Orange were hundreds of times greater than the levels considered safe by the US Environmental Protection Agency and caused thousands of deaths, many of them long after the war was over. In fact, Tetrachorodibenzodioxin has been described as "perhaps the most toxic molecule ever synthesised by man". Yet, over 75 million litres of this chemical herbicide/defoliant were sprayed over the forests of Vietnam, eastern Laos and parts of Cambodia and it is known to have caused birth defects, stillbirths and leukaemia in children of Vietnam veterans. Ten million hectares of agricultural land was destroyed in South Vietnam alone, partially achieving the purpose of degrading the ability of peasants to support themselves in the countryside and depriving guerrillas of their rural support base.

An interesting addendum from Wikipedia: "The Geneva Disarmament Convention of 1978, Article 2(4) Protocol III to the weaponry convention has 'The Jungle Exception', which prohibits states from attacking forests or jungles *'except if such natural elements are used to cover, conceal or camouflage combatants or military objectives or are military objectives themselves'*. This voids any protection of military or civilians from a napalm attack or something like Agent Orange and it is clear that it was designed to cater for situations like U.S. tactics in Vietnam. This clause has yet to be revised."

When sections of the trail were defoliated, the only way North Vietnamese cadres and trucks could continue to carry their loads south was to travel at night where they couldn't be seen by the helicopters and other aircraft searching for targets overhead. This made the journey even more perilous. During the day trucks had to be camouflaged with branches cut from trees or hidden wherever they could be obscured from the air, somctimes in caves.

As I ride, looking out and into the dark forest with its dense wall of trees, ferns the size of small houses, tangles of bamboo, vines, spiked grass, underbrush, I cannot stop my mind wondering about the lives of the soldiers on both sides of this senseless war: the Americans making their way stealthily through the tangle of forest, trying to keep off the trails for fear of mines, punji sticks buried at the bottom of concealed pits, booby traps, the point man setting the pace, eyes peeled, wondering when he would feel the bullets tear into him before he even heard the sound of a gun firing; the North Vietnamese and Viet Cong, readying themselves for a hit-and-run ambush or cooking their handful of rice on small fires before making camp for the night; or those cutting the route of the trail through the forest that would eventually stretch thousands of kilometres across this impossible terrain.

Somewhere to my left, deep in the forested cover of one of the hundreds of meaningless, nondescript, steep-sided hills that I ride past and over and around all day long, is Hamburger Hill.

I never found it or any of the other bases. In a way, I must admit that part of me didn't want to. The name itself, I find, is most unpleasant and demeaning towards those who were killed and maimed there. Human flesh torn apart and mangled by man-made explosives deserves a term more fitting, less flippant. But then, maybe being flippant was the only way some of the soldiers were able to stay sane, a coping strategy, keeping the horrors of war on the surface and not allowing them to penetrate too deep into the soul.

Densely covered with jungle, Hamburger Hill is an iconic example of the misguided "attrition" policy the Americans were following at the time. It ought to be stressed that the hill had no strategic significance whatsoever; it wasn't threatening anything or giving the enemy (or the US forces) any advantage. It was not - like the Khe Sanh Combat Base - part of a front line to be defended: it was just there, in the forest, just like thousands of similar steep-sided hills, thickly covered with nearly impenetrable jungle.

But the Americans wanted to provoke the North Vietnamese into a fight, get them to mass their forces against a defined target and then call in the artillery, the helicopter gun-ships, the bombers and kill as many of them as possible whilst attempting to reduce their own losses.

That was the basis of the war philosophy of "attrition" held at the time. The belief amongst the top brass was, to put it simply: If we can kill ten of the enemy for every one of our own, in the end they will give up, they will use up all their available men and the war will be won. A similar philosophy led to the slaughter at Passchendaele when General Haig tried (and failed) to "bleed the Germans white". As a consequence, in the mud of Flanders, the lives of some 245,000 British and 260,000 German soldiers were needlessly thrown away (although both figures are disputed. Some sources cite British casualties of between 325,000 - 400,000. But, hey, who's counting? Well, maybe the widows and children left behind?) Forgive my cynicism. I'm trying - and failing - to look at this dispassionately.

The battle for Ap Bia Mountain, designated Hill 937 by the US and later nicknamed "Hamburger Hill" was, in a way, the opposite of the battle for Khe Sanh. In the latter, the North Vietnamese were attacking an occupied and well-defended base whereas here, the US and PAVIN (People's Army of Vietnam) forces were attacking a hill occupied by well dug-in North Vietnamese troops. The battle was not on such a grand scale - it lasted only ten days to the 75 of Khe Sanh and fewer troops on both sides were involved. But it was the intensity of the fighting, the brutality which gave it its grotesque nickname, that has made this hill the most iconic of all the places of human slaughter in Vietnam.

The battle began on 10 May 1969. As always when US soldiers were involved in contact with the enemy, helicopter gun ships and artillery were called in to assist. But things went wrong almost immediately: the thick jungle made identifying targets for the supporting aircraft almost impossible and many US soldiers died from friendly fire while PAVIN forces occupying the higher slopes were bombed with napalm. After ten days the hill was finally taken. Some American units suffered over 60% casualties - 70 killed and 372 wounded. North Vietnamese casualties, as with all the battles throughout the war, large and small, are not known but, in keeping with the American fixation on keeping a tally, 630 bodies were collected afterwards.

In the Vietnam War, "body count" was the watchword - how many of ours and how many of theirs killed. So, according to the "body-count" theory, this battle was a resounding success - a ratio of 70:630, nearly ten to one. But it took the Americans a long time to realise that, for the North Vietnamese, it wasn't a matter of soldiers or civilians lost: it was a matter of winning the war and driving the hated invader out of their country. They would accept any number of casualties; America wouldn't. They'd done it before with the Chinese, the French, the Japanese. They would do it again... and again... until the foreign occupiers were driven out and they were free.

And so bloody was this battle that it led to the changing of US policy and affected public attitudes to the war, especially as, shortly after the hill had been taken with sickening loss of life, the Americans abandoned it and it was re-occupied by the North Vietnamese.

I realise that I am spending a large part of this narrative focusing on the war - weather it's called the "American" or "Vietnam" War, depending on the perspective one takes when reflecting on it - but, as I wrote in my introduction, to travel through this country as a tourist and merely take in its beauty without being aware of the bloody travails that its people have lived through over the centuries, the amount of blood that has soaked its soil, the leftover bombs and bits of bombs and shells and bullets and toxic chemicals and bodies and bits of bodies that hide under the roots of its vegetation, would be to insult the memory of all who fought and died here over the history of this place. I am aware of it every day as I ride, as I look into the faces of these gentle people who live their now peaceful lives with the quiet strength and stoicism that defines their race.

*****

What scared me most was that in Nam I became something that I am not. It called into question who I was and I was ashamed. I began to question my humanity. I'd fallen off the pedestal and I didn't like the person I had become. The war measured me and found me wanting. Me and my society. My foundation - all that I'd been taught in Sunday school, in church, by my parents - was gone. I was not that person any more. Where was my God in this? How could I live for the next fifty-sixty years with the memory of what we done? Of what I done?

A wall of exuberant life

At first, heading south, either side of the road is quite populated by hill people, their small wooden, stilted houses blending into the surrounding foliage. Children and chickens and dogs and cows make riding somewhat interesting. A man riding a scooter just in front of me hits a puppy and runs over it with both wheels. It writhes in the middle of the road, dying. He just rides on, not even pausing to look back. A disturbing image of running over a child comes to mind and, for a while, I ride more slowly - not that I've been riding particularly fast.

Of concern throughout this region is the disturbing evidence of forest destruction. Slash and burn is the accepted method of soil management in the high uplands regions of Vietnam. Huge swathes of forest have been cleared in this destructive way and the river, which follows the road, runs sluggish and yellow, clogged with soil eroded from the steep slopes, now denuded of their vegetative cover.

But as I enter deeper into the forest, still following the HCMT, the people disappear, the thick undergrowth that crowds the road seems untouched by the grubby hands of man until there are times when I feel as if I am the last person left on earth, that I have been permitted to remain for just a few hours more to ride this wonderful road alone, the forest and its endless curves for company.

Not wanting it to end and knowing that all too soon I will pass through these green-forested mountains into the dusty, smoke-filled land inhabited by human beings, I stop and switch off the engine.

The silence is profound, the smell of wet earth and vegetation heavy in the air. I need to get off the road, into that forest, feel it surround and encompass me, shut me in; experience, just for a few moments, the dense tangle of foliage in which so many soldiers from both sides fought and died.

I get off the bike and make my way to the forest edge, looking for a way in. I am confronted by a wall of exuberant life that knots and writhes in its desperate upward struggle for light and air and nutrients. Eventually I come across a narrow path, a trail leading into the thick undergrowth. I strip off my gear and scramble up a steep, muddy bank to the edge of the tree line then step inside.

The vegetation closes around me, presses against me with its warm, wet breath. I struggle to keep my footing. The path is steep and slick with mud. How a soldier, laden with so much kit and equipment that he struggles to stand - rifle, spare ammunition, grenades, side arm, food and personal kit, perhaps a radio or part of a disassembled machine gun and a belt or two of ammunition, Claymore mines for defence - could make his way through jungle this thick is impossible to imagine. To attack an enemy force, dug in and shooting down upon you, intent on killing you, whilst trying to climb a slope this steep, slippery and tangled with undergrowth...

It doesn't bear thinking about.

After only thirty metres or so the path disappears into the undergrowth and I am forced to stop. There is no way through. I retrace my steps to the road; the wet breath of the forest exhales me back into the empty world of human beings and my waiting bike.

By late evening I reach the town of Kham Duc. I have ridden today for 350ks through a thick-forested land of low mountains that continue on every side until the green covering foliage blues and merges with a hazy sky. The road, this legendary HCMT, seems to go on forever.

And resting in my room, I picture those undernourished, constantly harassed, ill soldiers in threadbare uniforms pushing their laden bicycles, carrying their loads along muddy tracks deep in this jungle, through rain and heat, across rivers, for months and months on end. And when they'd delivered their load, to turn back and do it all again.

And then again....

And, unlike the American soldiers who knew that, if they could just hang on for a year, they would be going home, the Vietnamese soldiers had no end to their war; it would end when it ended, not before.

Or when they died.

American soldiers were able to count the days to their release, like prisoners waiting for the metal doors to clang open. Their "real" world, the hedonistic world of America, seemed to continue unmindful of them in some parallel universe just a short flight away. Furthermore, it was unwritten policy that soldiers with just a few weeks left were not sent on dangerous missions so that the demoralising notion of someone being killed just days before the freedom of that final flight home did not lower morale. Despite the fact that most US soldiers fought valiantly in this unpopular war, many went through the motions, focused only on staying alive, doped themselves up to dull the horror of what they were being asked to do, to risk; and it is understandable why so many officers were "fragged" when the grunts under their leadership felt they were being led into a suicidal conflict.

The Vietnamese soldiers had nowhere they could fly to; weren't able to count the days...

* * * * *

A lot of guys cried in Nam and don't let no one tell you otherwise. A lot of guys who knows they dyin' cry, mostly they just sad and lonely, afraid to face the dark alone. No one want to be alone when they die. And their buddies, all tough and bad-ass as shit, look after them gentle like, speak to them like a baby or a girl, hold their hand, tell them it's going to be OK when they know it's not. Sometimes I'd get so I thought I couldn't take it no more, had to get out, and then I'd walk into the ward and see a guy with no legs feeding his buddy who's blind or whose hands are all bandaged up so he can't hold a spoon and I realise I have to stay. For them. If they can do that for their buddy then so can I. I can stay until I done my time.

Rice noodles and brutality

At 5.30 I am roughly awakened by a monotonous female voice counting out the moves for an early-morning Thai Chi class in the hall across the road. Her amplified voice is loud enough to wake the whole town. In enters my brain with the insistency of a metronome.

Outside my window the guesthouse sign is shorting out; it flickers on and off, on and off, seemingly keeping time with the woman's voice.

In this country there seems to be little understanding of the concept of auditory personal space. Everything must be loud: voices in a restaurant, speeches at a wedding, vehicle horns on the road, music from a karaoke den - all must be amplified until one winces, fearing permanent hearing loss.

I rouse myself, take pills for a headache and look out the window. The sky is clear. It's going to be hot.

I dress and head onto the street to look for food. Sometimes this can prove difficult.

Now I understand that when one travels through a foreign country it is only right that one partakes of the local food. Not to do so would be to deny oneself part of the cultural experience. The tastes and smells of exotic food, the sounds of a tongue foreign to one's ear, architectural peculiarities, clothing styles that speak of far-off lands, harsh desert landscapes or the wet exuberant foliage of the tropics - all these things make up the tapestry of a country, the things that excite our senses and remind us that we are travelling through someone else's land.

And where food is concerned, I realise that at times some might feel the need to eat a goat's eyeball, gnaw on a crispy locust or bite into the soft pussy flesh of a Mopane worm. Personally, I do not feel this need. It is my belief that certain foods are only eaten because, to the very poor and destitute, there is nothing else to available to sustain life. I don't need to eat a goat's eyeball to understand that some people do - and regard them as a delicacy. I'd rather remove the snake from its glass tank and set it free than watch while a grinning man cuts its throat and squeezes the blood into a glass for me to drink just so I can go home and tell all my friends that I have drunk snake blood, acting the intrepid traveller.

It is only natural that one gets used to one's own food and, after travelling for a while, the yearning for a plate of cereal, a ham roll, fish and chips, steak, egg and chips becomes overwhelming. I find, now, that I am eating only one meal a day because the very thought of eating noodles and slop (I realise I am being unkind here) for breakfast, noodles and slop for lunch and noodles and some meat (dog, perhaps?) and slop for supper takes my appetite away.

I just can't face watery noodles any more; I'd rather not eat at all.

I am, however, drinking a few cups of very strong coffee served with a finger of sweetened condensed milk each day and these alone ought to give my body a sufficiently large sugar and caffeine rush to last a few days. I know I'm already losing weight - but then that will probably allow me to blend in a little more with the stick-like body structure of most Vietnamese men.

Walking down the early-morning street, I find a small cafe opposite my guesthouse and order coffee. Opposite me a young man shovels laden chopsticks full of noodles into his mouth, biting off the pieces hanging out then sucking the soup from the bowl with contented slurpings. A dog with pendulous teats, heavily infested with mange, walks in off the street and looks for scraps between the tables. No one seems to mind.

My mind tells me I ought to eat but my stomach says no. Instead I order another coffee then relent and walk behind the counter into the kitchen to see what is there. In a pot are some bits of meat floating in weak gravy. I shake my head. Then I see some nuts in a jar and a bowl of salad leaves. I point to these and nod. The lady looks amused, a little confused, but I insist.

So I breakfast on coffee, salad and nuts, longing for a Full English or some cereal and fresh, cold milk.

Toast and marmalade, perhaps?

You just don't see bread on sale in the north or the central highlands. Or fresh milk. There are very few cows about and the only cereal crop that I have seen other than rice is the occasional small field of maize. So it's basically rice noodles or rice noodles.

Or nothing.

I pack up and continue on down Highway 14, through the forested hills and alongside rivers flowing blue-green and deep. The weather is good, the sky hot and clear.

Occasionally I come across Montagnard houses clustered in small groups in dense forest clearings. And, as I ride, I cannot but help allow my mind to dwell on the small bands of American soldiers coming upon villages just like these in the forest and searching them for hidden arms, treating the occupants with the contempt of their race, heavily armed and possessing within themselves the power of life and death. And whatever these hill people did or didn't do, they would suffer:

seen to be collaborating with the Americans, the VC would come back and kill them at night; any trace of a VC presence in the village or evidence that they might be supporting the VC in any way and the Americans would kill them during the day, burn down their houses, shoot their animals and destroy their crops.

And then there was the establishment of "kill zones" when an area of suspected VC penetration would be leafleted by helicopter, telling all those who lived or farmed in an area that as of a certain time and date anyone caught in this area would be considered the enemy and killed on sight. Some, especially the old, stayed, reluctant to leave their beloved homes and animals, the graves of their ancestors; some younger ones would remain behind to look after them and they would all end up being killed.

Burn someone's home, kill their livestock, desecrate the graves of their ancestors, destroy their crops and you might, for a time, deny succour to the enemy, the VC cadres roaming the forest at night, the North Vietnamese soldiers making their slow way south; but even if the war is won, you will create a bitterness and resentment that will last generations.

So much for hearts and minds.

That is a lesson the Brits had to learn long ago during the Boer War in South Africa when, trying to fight a guerrilla war against those hardy, khaki-clad Afrikaner farmers with their deadly Mauser rifles and their indomitable spirit, they cleared the farms, burned down the farmsteads, killed the cattle and sheep, interned the women and children in what is generally recognised as the first ever use of concentration camps. Thousands died of disease and despair behind the barbed wire fences. Rumours circulated that the Brits were deliberately killing them, feeding them ground glass with their meagre rations. This, despite being untrue, has never been forgotten by succeeding generations of Afrikaners who, generally, bear ill will towards anything or anyone British.

In this country there ought to be a great deal of bitterness towards foreigners - especially Americans. Yet there doesn't seem to be. I certainly never experienced it.

These are a forgiving people.

*****

I saw a lot of the pilots fly drunk. They'd come in and head for the bar and drink, just to get by, just to cope with all the stuff they seen out there or done. That or drugs. Most were on marijuana. Some on the harder stuff. Some doctors came back addicted to heroin. I seen them come in, get out the aircraft and puke their guts out. Gunships, medivacs, nurses whatever. It made no difference. They did what it took to get by out there, to cope. Everybody have their own way to cope.

F*** the Government

Travelling from Kham Duc in the highlands towards Pleiku, the road descends from over 1000m onto a plateau about 500m high. The hills are lower and less steep, the population massively increased. As I descend, the temperature rises until I am baking in the high thirties. My European skin is not designed for this and begins to crisp. The bike seems to have no power - or less than the paltry amount it usually offers - and I am convinced it is over heating.

Kon Tum, capital of the province with the same name, my trusty out-of-date guide book tells me, is a place to "avoid the beaten track"; a sleepy town inhabited mainly by Montagnards, on the original (and seldom travelled) Ho Chi Minh Trail.

I was looking forward to a rest there; sit quietly in the shade of a tree, stilted houses nestling in palm-shrouded glades, the well-trodden remnants of "the Trail" disappearing into the thick surrounding underbrush. I'd commune with friendly hill people, the women dressed in their richly-decorated garb, absorb the atmosphere, allow my mind to travel back in time...

However, when I eventually reach it, hot, sweaty and sun-burned, it turns out to be little more than another dirty, stinking hot, bustling city/town with nary a Montagnard in sight. Perhaps since the publication of my guidebook they have all moved away. Not only are there no Hill People, tragically there is no forest either.

It's gone. Destroyed. Flattened. Burned.

The surrounding hills are bare with just an occasional tree left standing, exposed and vulnerable, the soil washing away from its roots. The red soil is all in the rivers now, so thick with it that the flow has become sluggish and hesitant.

This environmental tragedy is being played out all through the highlands here in Vietnam but also throughout the world where virgin tropical forests so vital to our survival as a species are being cut, slashed and burned for some specious short-term gain. We are sleepwalking towards widespread habitat destruction and inevitable climate change, which will alter the nature of this planet. The defoliation of these forests by the Americans with Agent Orange was a conscious, immoral decision; but allowing their destruction through inefficiency and political lethargy is something just as bad.

I ride through the cool shadow of a tunnel. Spray painted on the entrance wall are the words: "F*** the government, save the forests."

I think that just about sums it up.

Disappointed in Kon Tum, I press on in the heat to Pleiku, the hillsides denuded of all natural vegetation the whole way. Now consider this: the road I have been travelling along was once an integral part of the original HCMT, a trail that had to have been routed through dense forest to enable supplies to be moved unseen from the air. Logically, then, one must assume that this area, just over forty years ago, was fully covered with a layer of natural tropical forest so dense that it enabled the soldiers carrying their loads of ammunition and supplies, their laden bicycles, the heavy trucks, to move unseen from the air for thousands of kilometres. Had this not been so, they would soon have been picked off by helicopter gunships like rats in a barrel.

No, dense tropical forest once covered these hills and it has, sadly, been destroyed by the rape of slash-and-burn in a short four decades...

By late afternoon I reach the town of Pleiku.

Of some historical interest: "In February 1965 the VC shelled a US compound in Pleiku, killing eight Americans. Although the USA already had more than 23,000 military advisers in Vietnam, their role was supposed to be non-combative at the time. The attack on Pleiku was used as a justification by President Johnson to begin a relentless bombing campaign against North Vietnam and the rapid build-up of US troops.

"When US troops departed in 1973, the South Vietnamese kept Pleiku as their main combat base in the area. When these troops fled the advancing VC, the whole civilian population of Pleiku and nearby Kon Tum fled with them. The stampede to the coastline involved over 100,000 people, but tens of thousands died along the way.

"The departing soldiers torched Pleiku, but the city was rebuilt in the 1980s with assistance from the Soviet Union." Vietnam - Lonely Planet

After washing my clothes and showering the road dust from my skin, I take my evening perambulation into the city looking for food and a beer.

Gracious people - so very different from the stiff reserve one finds in Britain. Everywhere I go, I am greeted. Not the slightly mocking, "Hey, you!" that often follows strangers in foreign places, but sincere greetings delivered with a smile. Small children call after me and giggle; two young men invite me to take a slice of mango they are eating off the bonnet of a car... I stop at a cafe to have yet another cup of coffee and a middle-aged man, slight but with powerful looking hands and forearms, invites me to share his table. He is the only one there and speaks no English so we sit in quietly together and sip our slowly percolating coffee. A little later the young lady who served me brings a pot of tea and two small bowls, as is the tradition, and the silent man with powerful hands ceremoniously prepares tea for both of us.

One expects this sort of thing in a small, rural setting, a village where there are few people about; but in a city...

* * * * *

It wasn't no main road. It was like a old dirt trail. There was a minesweeper in front of us. Then a couple of tanks. We was fourth in line, the last vehicle. We hit this mine. Got blew up. Blew the track straight up in the air.

I thought it was all over. When that thing blew up, I never heard nothin' like that before in my life. That was the loudest sound I ever heard in my life. It blew us right off the track.

When I came down, the track fell on my leg. We didn't have the cover on it you put over the top if it rains. If that would've been on, we would've got trapped in there. I don't know whether the shotgunner got killed or not. He was on the other side with his machine gun.

I was just burnin' up. I was burnin' everywhere. It ain't no gas stations in the field. You run out of gas, you just run out of gas. It no tellin' when somebody might come by and bring you some. So we had these gas cans with us. They must've exploded too. Fire was runnin' all up my fatigues. Somethin' just keep tellin' me, Pull your leg out. Pull your leg out. My left leg. I was steady diggin' and steady tryin' to get it out, and I finally got it out. I just nearly tore my right hand off.

I was never taught to roll over when you on fire, and I start runnin'. And that's what I did wrong. It felt like I was in hell. I was just screamin' and screamin'. So the guy that was in the tank in front of me told me to lie down, and he put it out with the stuff they carry.

So they had me sittin' on the side of the road waitin' for the helicopter. It must have took 20 minutes. They gave me something. Maybe morphine, and I sort of passed out. I had third-degree burns everywhere. The skin was just hangin' off my left arm. My right arm was burned completely to the bone. My face was all burnt up. It was white. I caught gangrene in my right hand, and they took the thumb off. The hand just kept getting bigger and bigger. Finally my doctor told me that he had to take it off, because gangrene was getting ready to go all through my body.

Well, I didn't want to die. So they cut it off.

From "Bloods" by Wallace Terry

Hoping to witness an execution

I punch tomorrow's route into my GPS. The machine does something strange: on my map, the route south is clear and obvious, a thick red line heading from Pleiku to Ea Drang, Buon Ma Thuot and the south west towards the Cambodian border to Dak Mil where I plan to spend the night. Instead, somewhat perversely, it - well, "she", the wilful woman who lives in my GPS - has chosen to divert me along a small track that isn't even dignified with the addition of colour. At least there are *two* thin black lines on the map and not just one. It seems to follow the Cambodian border all the way south for 200ks before making its way onto larger roads to Saigon/Ho Chi Minh City.

Who am I to argue? She's a woman after all. The road/track will take me alongside the area where US and North Vietnamese forces were involved in their first major conflict in 1965. I'm excited. The road not taken and all that.

Marked on the map with the number 14C, it's clearly a more remote branch of the HCMT, one of the spurs further east and close to the border with Cambodia; easier to escape across when attacked by a superior US force during the early part of the war when the Americans still respected the Cambodian and Laotian borders. This would change.

Shortly after setting off from Pleiku, I take a small road east. It is narrow and becomes increasingly pot-holed. After passing through dusty villages that cluster about the main road, I enter an empty land, flattish and scrubby. The road loses its crumbling tar and becomes a dirt track. My speed drops and the temperature climbs until I am forced to stop and strip off some gear; I ride on without helmet and gloves, sacrificing safety for the feel of hot air passing over my skin.

Now this is what motorcycle travel is all about, I think to myself, loving it, the wild remoteness of it, the red dust from the road billowing behind me; it's the kind of road that makes you want to slow down just to preserve the moment a little longer.

I am somewhere near the Cambodian border. I don't quite know where but that is of no consequence. The road is good dirt, some lumps and bumps, layered with a centimetre of fine red dust, occasional corrugations and longer sections of bull dust that need to be treated with respect. No vehicles - I lie, there was one truck but it was parked so that doesn't count. A few scooters. Chickens that seem to prefer the companionability of the road whenever I come across crudely built wooden houses. The occasional pig or two.

As I press further west, though, it becomes a devastated landscape, black with burning, the stumps of trees standing in mute rebuke like those iconic shattered trees left standing in the mud after the battle of the Somme. In places trees still burn, the air hazed and acrid with the smoke of their dying.

The heat is oppressive. I come across a small village and stop, switch off the engine and feel the heat gather around me like a presence, like some hot, living thing leaning itself against me. As I write this, I sit, shirtless, at a small table under a crude veranda, roofed with corrugated iron. My coffee is dripping in front of me, the tin of condensed milk and glass of ice waiting to be mixed. A pot-bellied pig waddles past through the dust, pauses to munch on a discarded banana. Outside, everything is white in the harsh light, leached of all colour. The good woman who has brought me coffee, seeing I am suffering in the heat, brings a fan and sets it on a plastic chair in front of me, directs a tepid stream of air onto my body. She then wets the floor by flicking water from a plastic bucket and at last I am cool.

Two men call to me from another rambling wooden shack, shaded under leafy trees. I walk into the oven of air, cross the road to talk with them. Well, "talk" is a little generous: we speak a few words to each other in our own languages and smile and that passes for acceptable phatic communication.

They are wild looking fellows. One is a little drunk, I fear.

Standing in the dirt road is what passes in the remoter regions of Vietnam as a tractor, truck, prime mover - the first of this kind I have seen. Little more than a one-cylinder engine, open flywheel, similar to the vintage engines my son Gareth used to restore in South Africa - Bamford and Petta, Lister, Briggs and Stratton - bolted onto a rigid steel frame. Only two wheels, no gearbox, the drive taken through three massive fan belts attached directly to the flywheel. Bolted onto the front, a powerful winch, also fan-belt driven. Because it has only two wheels, to function it has to be connected to a trailer. The driver sits on a hunk of hardwood a foot square in front of a large steering wheel. Robust technology from the early 20th century, over-engineered and with few moving parts, easy to repair in some backyard workshop with a few spanners and a hammer.

I stand in the heat of the sun and admire this primitive beast, stripped to the essentials - engine, wheels, winch, steering wheel - and love the honesty of it.

Its owner approaches me. I indicate my admiration of his primitive steed and he smiles, walks to the side of the engine and, putting all his weight into the action, cranks it into life. The air is filled with a blue oil-haze, the clatter of the single piston loud in the still air.

Back at my small plastic table, I sip my coffee knowing that this is why I have come. To discover Vietnam, to meet with its people.

Now I know, of course, that city people are also Vietnamese, but the bustle and the noise, the concrete, the scream of a thousand scooters and the ugly blare of truck horns through a dirty urban sprawl becomes trying after a while and one longs for the slower pace of wild, out-of-the-way places. And I have found it, just this small patch of sun-baked land, for this short time. I have, briefly, opened the veil that separates the traveller from the people, and stepped inside.

And it is good...

Outside the shade of the veranda, the sun beats down with a white-hot intensity, reflecting off the dust of the road.

Time to head on, I fear.

With the bitter-sweet taste of coffee still lingering in my mouth, I make my way to my bike where a group of men and women have congregated, as they always do in places like this, interested in this stranger who has appeared into their midst and who will disappear again after a short half hour and leave no trace of his passing but a tenuous memory. The men have been poking at my GPS, staring at my strapped-on luggage, commenting on this and that. The drunk man attempts to put on my helmet and I help him, much to the amusement of the watchers. He wants to get on the bike but I shake my head and restrain him. He reluctantly gives me back my helmet and I mount up, start the bike and ride up the red-dust street at peace with myself and the world.

I make another twenty or so kilometres before I pause to investigate a stripped-down logging truck on the roadside, 4X4, V8 and cab-less, winch-driven crane constructed from a 6-inch pipe pivoted on a hunk of metal protruding from the front of the chassis. Another utilitarian beast of the outback, stripped to its essentials.

I am concentrating on taking a photograph when a man calls out to me. He leans out of the window of his car and at first I do not understand what he wants of me.

Is it the camera? I know this is a politically sensitive area, close to the Cambodian border, a place denied to all foreigners just a short while ago.

He beckons me over. He shows me his ID and I realise that he is a policeman. He asks me to follow him.

I get back on my bike and ride behind his car in a cloud of red dust that hangs in the still air. We leave the village behind.

I am not overly concerned: he has a kind face.

At the station - a sprawling, single-story house with a wide, corrugated-iron-roofed veranda closed in on three sides - I am invited to sit on one side of a long wooden table. Despite the shade, it is hot. The policeman brings me a glass of water, which I take as a good sign. He could have poured it over my face while it was covered with a piece of cloth. He has a few words of English. I hand him my passport. He peruses each page with methodical interest then copies all my details into a ledger. It's a slow process. I am sure he copies each letter by its shape.

A crowd has gathered in the road outside and they stare at me. They stand in the sun and the stark light makes them look pale and insubstantial. I get the feeling they are watching with morbid interest an arrested criminal, hoping to witness an execution.

All the while, my policeman is making phone calls on his mobile. I have the unpleasant notion that he is speaking to someone high up, saying something like, "We've got this British chap on a bike close to the border with Cambodia. Looks a bit dodgy. Do I lock him up?"

He indicates that he wants to know where I'm going so I go to the bike to get my map. The gathered crowd of silent watchers opens to let me through. Back in the muggy darkness of the veranda, I unfold the map, lay it on the table and trace my proposed route south along the Cambodian border.

He shakes his head and a look of disappointment comes over his face.

Just then a middle-aged man who speaks passable English arrives. The phone calls, I assume. He, too, looks at the map, traces his finger along the route I plan to take then he tells me that it is impossible.

"Why?" I ask, disappointed.

"The road... closed," he tells me. "The bridge - you know - it is down. To get across the river - not possible."

I ask about the bridge and I think he tells me it went down in 1964, but I might be mistaken. Pesky Americans dropping bombs...

I want to go on and see the bridge, try to get across the river in something that floats but feel that I would be pushing my luck. Reluctantly I bid my policeman friend and his translator goodbye, make my way through the spectators who look disappointed that they are not to watch a lynching, and fire up the bike. It takes me a while to find my way back to the original road and I wander along narrow tracks through the bush for a while, slithering through patches of soft sand.

Then, disappointed, I retrace my steps to the main, tarred HCMT, Highway 14, and continue heading south.

* * * * *

I had a dog in Vietnam. His name was Pussy. In Nam, you know you have a capacity to love, but there was no one else in the fucking world that loved you. The only thing I could love while I was there was a God damn dog. So I was very close to Pussy.

We had a rat epidemic and rabies, so they were going round killing all the dogs. There was a bitch named Ralph that had had puppies at Christmas. When the MP was killing all the dogs at the base camp, he shot Ralph's nose off. Ralph ran down the road and we had to hit her over the head with a shovel to kill her. I said to myself that there was no way this was going to happen to Pussy. When the MP came to kill Pussy, I just yanked back the bolt on my M-16 and said, "What do you want?"

"I've come for your dog," he said.

"No, you haven't. You've come for me."

"No, I just want to shoot the dog." He wore gloves and was shooting them with a .45.

"I'll tell you what," I said. "Shoot the dog. I shoot you. That's the situation. Go ahead. There's the dog." He walked away.

From "Nam" by Mark Baker

Circus performers desperate to make a living

By the time I finally manage to retrace my steps to the main road it is already after midday; the heat is even more oppressive. I debate with myself whether to give up this attempt to follow the small dirt road and just do the tar thing, take the easy option south but I decide to give it one more try. There is a maze of small dirt tracks between the main Highway 14 and the border with Cambodia and one of them must be able to lead me onto my original track south of the downed bridge.

Eventually, I discover another track heading east then south and take it. Immediately it is clear that this is something different. Whereas my first attempt was along a clean but narrow road making its way through pleasant countryside, this road is somehow ugly in a compelling sort of way. The broken tar soon gives way to a dirt track deep red in colour, covered with a layer of bull dust that at times must be all of six inches deep. At first, the roadside and surrounding scrubland is covered in filth, bushes and trees festooned with the fluttering remnants of discarded plastic bags. Soon the bike, my clothes and luggage are stained red with a fine layer of dust that gathers in the corners of my mouth and eyes and clings to the sweat of my body. The further east I ride, the more the road deteriorates - rocks, steep dips and gullies, hard-shouldered tracks worn through the surface that threaten to have me over. The going is slow.

But at last, as I leave humanity behind, the litter thins and disappears. It is as if the land has wiped its hands clean of the smudge of humanity and suddenly it is beautiful again. A stark, remote beauty, hot and dusty, a land of trees and rocks and ragged shrubs that mute themselves into the smoky haze of the horizon, the cloudless sky above wide and white with heat. I begin to enjoy the challenge of the road again, the feel of the tyres slewing and undulating through soft sand. I stop and remove my helmet and gloves again, strap them on top of my luggage and allow the hot wind to touch my skin.

Small Montagnard settlements begin to appear; the stilted houses no longer quaint and picturesque, surrounded by the deep green of bamboo and banana trees; here they are run down, covered like everything else with a fur of red dust. The men who lounge about wear worn clothes, their faces and limbs gaunt as if just keeping alive in this place is a struggle. Each decaying settlement seems to be engaged in slashing and burning so that the air is acrid with smoke. In places I ride through a scrubby landscape that is still on fire and I feel the heat of the flames against my skin. The earth is grey with ash and stumps continue to smoulder long after the fire has passed. I don't see any ploughed fields, though, just a burned-out land.

Logging continues in this place, harvesting what is left of the big trees that once covered this ground with a soft, wet canopy, a concealing camouflage of foliage, now destroyed. It's not large-scale logging, rich multi-nationals with expensive machinery, bulldozers with linked chains ripping up the land. This is more low tec but, in the end, just as devastating.

I first become aware of how cut logs are transported from the forest closer to the main road when I see something strange making its way towards me along the dusty track. Its motion is slow and rolling, like a small boat on an undulating sea. Intrigued, I stop and switch off the engine. The thing approaches with a ponderous heaviness, another behind it and, even further back, another.

When the first is close enough, I realise that each of these things is a small motorbike, what in my youth we called "buzz-bikes", pressed-steel body, 50cc engines. Strapped across the puny frame at right angles are two heavy poles, 6-9 inches in diameter, to create a carrying frame. Strapped onto these are four massive split logs, seven or so metres in length, two on either side of the seat. The rider has to step inside the two sets of logs in order to ride.

How these small bikes do not collapse immediately under a load so preposterous I have no idea. The weight and length of the logs protruding metres in front of and behind the wheels makes for the wallowing motion over the rough track. How they keep the bikes up, how they manage to escape having their legs crushed by the logs if - and when, surely - they fall...

Perhaps they don't. Perhaps the bikes do fall apart, the logs do crush legs in a fall, but no one cares.

I ride on, filled with a deep admiration for these people and what they are able to achieve with so little, for their resilience and skill.

A short while later I come across a small settlement where four of these laden bikes are parked to one side of the road, their riders sitting under the shade of a Montagnard stilted home drinking coffee. I stop, dismount and check out the bikes. I need to know how toy motorcycles manufactured for teenagers are able to carry such heavy loads without breaking apart. On closer inspection I can see that the frames have been strengthened with pieces of flat bar and reinforcing rod welded across the stress points, but the basic pressed steel frame - like the exoskeleton of a beetle - is unchanged. Any engineer would condemn them immediately as inherently unsafe; would predict metal fatigue, cracking and frame collapse. A Health and Safety officer would begin taking names...

And yet the little bikes nod their awkward, lumbering way along this execrable track day after day, delivering hand-split logs to the highway where they can be picked up by large trucks and delivered to where ever. And these stick-limbed Vietnamese men, gaunt and smiling, ride them like un-funny circus performers desperate to make a living.

Seeing me scrutinising their bikes, four men leave their coffee and the shade of the veranda and approach me. They are hardy, rough-looking men yet the welcome in their smiles removes any momentary concern I might have for my safety. We have no shared language at all so I point to the welded struts holding the frames together, to the massive logs strapped onto their bikes, the dilapidated state of them, and laugh, throwing my hands into the air and shaking my head. They laugh too, understanding. They look at my bike, prod the GPS and mutter to each other. I demonstrate its capabilities. They nod in appreciation.

They invite me by pointing and miming to share coffee with them but it is getting late and I gesture my thanks and mount my bike. It is with sadness that I leave these gnarled men, their smooth skin turned orange with dust, and ride away on my own into the smoky late-afternoon light.

The road continues to worsen. I ride through a burnt land, larger logs and stumps still smouldering, the ash thick on the ground. In places, close to the road, the fire burns with a shocking heat but I see no one responsible for it or controlling it in any way. It seems so randomly destructive.

On a steep, rocky corner I come across one of those utilitarian, two-wheeled tractors tethered to a trailer upon which is lashed an impossibly heavy load of newly-cut logs. The driver, a young man barely out of his teens and wearing a baseball cap, sits on his box just behind the engine. The logs hem him in on both sides. He is unconcerned, resting one arm nonchalantly on a log while he controls the fan belts that act as a clutch between the engine and wheels.

Five other sweating men in dusty clothes walk alongside the machine. Just opposite me one of the trailer wheels gets wedged behind a large rock in the road; the tractor comes to a halt, both driving wheels continuing to grind away, flinging up dust. The engine hardly hesitates. Alternately engaging and disengaging the clutch belts, the young driver allows the tractor to roll back then forward again but each time the rock flings him back. The wheels start digging through the hard surface clay of the road, bedding down, and I can see it's not going to move. Then the walking men all get behind the trailer and push; one carries a steel bar longer than he is tall and uses it as a lever behind the trailer wheels. Eventually with a thump it climbs the rock and, with a wave to me, they continue on their way, obscured by a cloud of blue smoke.

A little later I drop the bike attempting a u-turn on a steepish, rocky section of road and, by the time I lift it, I am dripping sweat and covered in dust.

Tired now and dirty, I press on towards a small town in the middle of nowhere called Ea Sup, reaching it as the sun sinks red beneath the horizon.

I ride slowly through the streets, looking for a hotel or guesthouse sign, knowing that the likelihood of finding such a luxury in the middle of nowhere is remote. Faced with the prospect of riding another 150ks in the dark to reach the next town, I stop and ask two young women who direct me to a small hotel tucked down a side street where I collapse onto the bed, feeling a little ill. Eight hours of burning sun, riding in this heat has taken it out of me. I am concerned about heat stroke but soon I begin to recover and am able to wash the sweat and dust off my skin and clothes. Time to look for a cold one and, perhaps, something to eat that isn't rice noodles.

Later, cold beer in hand, a thin straggle of traffic passing desultorily on the road in front of me, I study the map of South Vietnam and find a route that might take me back to the Cambodian border, back onto road 14C with the downed bridge. It does lead through the Yok Don National Park so I hope important-looking bits of paper festooned with official stamps are not required. That will take me to Dak Mil, if you're interested. Then from there it's head down to Ho Chi Minh City.

As the beer - horrible stuff but ridiculously cheap - mellows my soul, I feel satisfied that I didn't take the easy option and stay on the tar. Tar roads are little more than... well, tar roads. It's the small tracks upon which the memories, like layers of dust, cling.

My journey - and others before this - has been all the richer for these beaten-up tracks: the heat, the bull dust and the brief connection with a small group of hardy men riding over-loaded buzz-bikes.

* * * * *

Most of the nightmares are gone. Except one.

I still think about this North Vietnamese soldier. We took two hours to kill him. This was a brave dude. I'll never forget him. It took a whole platoon to kill him.

He was held up in a tunnel. He knew he had no possible chance of winning whatsoever. And he wasn't really expecting no help. But this was the bravest dude I had ever seen. And I respect this dude.

The "rabbits", they were so crazy they didn't understand nothing, see. We had interpreters to rap to him to give up. If he give up, they would rehabilitate him and shit like that. And he would fight for the regular Vietnamese army. They rapped and rapped to him. And we started shooting and throwing frags and Willie Peter rounds - white phosphorous grenades that burn through metal and shit.

But the only way we got him was this crazy rabbit jumped down in the hole and beat him to the punch. With a shotgun right through his neck. So when they pulled him out, he was hit badder than an ol' boy. He had a hunk of meat out of his leg, big as that. He had shrapnel all over his body. He had a hole in his side. But he wouldn't give up. Because he really believed in something. This man was willing to die for what he believed in. That was the first time I ran into contact with a real man. I will never forget him.

From "Bloods" by Wallace Terry

Risk it or turn back

Time moves slowly in this place, as slow as the drips of coffee that make their way through the filter and, drop by tiny drop, into the finger of thick, sweetened condensed milk in the bottom of the glass. There's no hurrying it; you just wait until, some fifteen minutes later, the level of black is twice the depth of the creamy white, like the Guinness ads only the other way round. During this time you sit quietly and contemplate the passing scene, pour yourself a glass of black tea which is always served with the coffee, and generally be sociable with those sitting around in a similar state of waiting. When the last drop has separated itself from the filter and the slow ripples have stilled, you remove the aluminium filter from the glass, place it in its lid, stir up the mixture and pour it over the glass of ice that's been waiting, condensation beading on its surface.

Not so the street markets. They are always frenetic. I stumbled upon yet another yesterday evening as I was out on my usual constitutional in search of beer and something to eat. Stalls spill out into both sides of the road; the narrow gap between is filled with a seething mass of humanity and scooters, all busily making their way somewhere, a turbulent swirl of moving life that, somehow, doesn't tangle or fray. At my feet, in the middle of the road (where I am forced to walk because the stall owners have claimed the pavements) a dogfish stares balefully at me with its protuberant eyes and a slightly puzzled expression on its face. While I ponder the incongruity of a live fish looking at me from the hot surface of the road, a woman with a plastic bowl deftly scoops him up and deposits him in a larger bowl full of water with the other dog-fish. He had chosen the moment of her distraction to escape.

Large, mud-coloured frogs tied together in pairs with string around their waists look resigned. If only they could coordinate their leaps, they might make a bid for freedom. Crabs (those horrible little black ones children throw back into muddy water after dipping their baited strings into rivers), shrimp, octopus, shellfish in plastic buckets. Large, bewiskered catfish gasp for air in shallow aluminium bowls, air pumped through thin pipes keeping them vaguely alive until they are bought and killed. Ducks, chickens, pigeons in cages, meat being chopped into hunks with cleavers on wooden chopping boards; intestines, pigs' ears, trotters, heads, gutted and plucked birds spread-eagled and waxy yellow. Fish, newly-killed, are de-scaled and gutted by thin women with blood-slick hands who crouch in gutters and smile at me as I pass. The blood pools and flies gather. A plastic bag on the end of a stick serves as a handy flywhisk and women crouch on their haunches behind the displayed meat and waft away insistent flies with a rhythmic boredom. Puppies in cages look pathetic and endearing. (I hope they are not being sold for the table.) Bunches of bananas, coconuts, roots of strange, contorted, underground things I never knew existed. Eggs of various sizes. Fruit. Small stalls selling fast food, Vietnamese style. Charcoal burners haze the air with smoke and the smell of its burning. Eels writhe and knot themselves in an inch of water. In amongst the edibles, brightly-coloured, cheap plastic things from China; motorcycle repair shops; hardware...

In a wardrobe-sized room just off the road a young woman shaves off my beard with a blunt cut-throat razor and, when the blade scrapes past my jugular vein, I cannot help thinking of the GIs who, after a particularly fierce night attack on their compound, found the Vietnamese man who owned the local barber shop dead on the wire wearing the black pyjamas favoured by the VC.

I ask for a beer at a roadside place and they bring it to me in a glass with a straw. It turns out to be sugar cane juice. Not what I had hoped, but its cloying sweetness is refreshing. On the telly, over-acted re-runs of embarrassingly bad kung fu movies play, the volume turned up loud. An older woman crouches at my side, pats herself between her legs and laughs a mouthful of bad teeth at me. I assume she is offering a service.

As I leave, a heavy-set man calls me over to his table and insists I drink with him. Politeness compels me to agree although I would prefer to be on my way. I sit while he pours me a glass of some clear liquid that, when I drink it, makes my eyes water...

But I get ahead of myself. The day...

I badly want to try again to get onto the small border road, Route 14C, feel the dust of a section of the original Ho Chi Minh Trail under my tyres again, uncovered by the civilizing influence of tar. My map shows a small road to the east that will join yesterday's aborted attempt somewhere below the broken bridge. I punch it into my GPS and head off. After about fifty kilometres it leads me into a small village and onto a concrete ramp that disappears into the dark, slow moving waters of a river. On the other side I can see a similar concrete ramp emerging from the water and becoming a road of sorts that makes its way through the dusty bush. Pulled up onto the muddy riverbank on my side are some narrow canoes large enough to take my bike.

While I look about for someone to ask, a soldier carrying an AK47 over his shoulder arrives on the back of a scooter. I watch him, assuming that if he is able to get across the river then so can I. But, no, he walks off. I call after him and ask whether I can cross with the bike. He shakes his head.

"How can I get across?" I ask him.

The tells me in broken English that there is a bridge two kilometres to the south and, filled with hope, I set off on what will turn out to be three hours of fruitless attempts to get across the river that blocks my way to the east.

I follow a dirt track which heads in the right direction; after a few kilometres I can see the river again but this time the track leads me onto a low, temporary bridge made of poles, the broken bits covered with loose wooden planks. Filled with expectation, I cross and struggle up the steep, sandy bank on the other side. Over a ridge and there, in front of me, is the real river, wider than it was in the village. Just to one side, knee-deep in reeds, a herd of elephant graze.

I have crossed nothing more than a small tributary. I turn back, re-cross the bridge and continue out of town, exploring every side road until, inevitably, it too comes to a stop against the implacable river barrier or turns and heads away in another direction. At one time I bump my way across a newly ploughed field, through patches of soft sand until I reach an equally un-crossable river. There are no boats.

In the end I give up and make my way on the tar road south towards Duc Lap. Mind in neutral, my flesh melting in the heat, I resign myself to running down the miles. And then, just before I reach Duc Lap, a small voice insinuates itself into my heat-numbed brain: If I can't get onto road 14C from the north and ride it across bombed bridges and slow-green rivers from N to S, what's to stop me riding it S to N - well, at least until I meet another river or downed bridge. But then, it's getting late; I'm tired and sweaty and have been bumbling around following small dirt roads to nowhere all day; a shower and a cold beer are calling...

But I slow and make a U-turn. Take out the map. I find a small road that heads east and joins road 14C that looks do-able. The turn-off is only about eight kilometres back.

As soon as I am off the main road and onto a narrow, pot-holed track, my spirits lift. Even the air feels cooler, although that might be because the sun is lowering on the horizon. I am travelling again, exploring, not merely enduring. It's the journey, not the destination that counts, they say - and they're right. The evening settles to that strange calm that seems to come over the land with the dying of the sun, and the trees and the grass and the dust of the road take upon themselves a three-dimensional brightness. There are no cars, not even a scooter to shatter the evening calm. I pass one of those strange two-wheeled, stripped-down prime movers pulling a trailer and spewing diesel fumes. The driver waves.

And then it's just me and the road and the bush. The tar has broken up long ago and I ride across a good surface of dirt whose colour and texture reflects the geology below: deep red, smooth sand, blindingly white chalk that billows behind me like a sheet flapping in the wind. There are rocky patches and long stretches of bull dust that I cross with care because there's no knowing what lies beneath its powdery surface that flows through one's fingers like water. I ride into a section of tall trees, not yet obliterated by the slash-and-burn vandals, the road suddenly dark with shade. A mile stone: underneath the stone-battered white paint I can just make out: QL 14C. I've finally made it.

The track forks. No signs. I take the left, the one that will lead me closer to Cambodia rather than back into Vietnam. It forks again and then again. I choose tracks at random, whichever looks the most appealing in the few seconds I have to make a decision.

Then, half obscured by bush, I notice a sign: BORDER BELT. I pause and think: Go on and risk it or turn back?

But I'm having such fun.

I fire up the bike and press on... just one more corner. And another. And then another...

My luck runs out. A soldier wearing camouflage and carrying a firearm stands in the middle of the road and flags me down.

One corner too many...

I stop, switch off the engine and remove my helmet. Smile and act normal, as if you've just met an acquaintance on a street corner. All good here, mate - and you? Ignore the uniform and the gun.

He's friendly. Points into the bush towards Cambodia and says something in Vietnamese. I know exactly what he's saying but act ignorant and frame a question with my face. He pulls out his mobile phone, flicks to Gallery and shows me a photograph. There's no doubt that the picture he's selected is of the sign half covered by underbrush that I've just ignored, telling me I'm about to enter a border area.

I look shocked. Me? In a border area? Goodness, how on earth did that happen! I place my hands together in the universal sign of peace and submission, swirl my hand above my head to indicate a U-turn and put my helmet back on in a businessman-like fashion. He doesn't point his gun at me, doesn't grip me firmly by the upper arm. He backs away, job done, and I quickly turn the bike and retrace my steps, relieved. Being arrested would have been an inconvenience. I ride fast just in case he was heading back to his tent in the bush not to sleep or play cards but to phone ahead for someone in authority to arrest me before I reach the main road.

No one stops me and, as I ride fast through the darkening trees, I am pleased that I decided to make the effort to find this road. First, for the sheer pleasure of it but also because it reassured me that, even if I had made it across the river further north (and, had I the time, I have no doubt I would have been able to find someone who would ferry me across for a small fee) I would have been stopped before long by gun-toting soldiers manning a check-point and guarding their border with Cambodia.

Back on the main tar road, I ride another 60ks before reaching the town of Gia Nghia and finding a hotel vaguely reminiscent of the worst that the ex-Soviet Union can offer.

Later that night it begins to rain - fat, heavy drops that strike the corrugated iron outside my window like flung marbles. The whole world smells of warm, wet earth.

* * * * *

I remember one night I put my little transistor radio on my pack. We listened to music with the earphones, and he talked about his wife and kids back home on the farm in Georgia. He said he would be glad to see is wife.

The next day he was walking point. I was walking the third man behind him when he hit a booby trap. I think it was a 104 round. It blew him up in the air about 8 feet. He came down, and about an inch of flesh was holding his leg to his body. He rested on his buttocks, and his arms were behind him. He was moaning and crying in agony and pain and stuff. What really got to his mind is when he rose himself up and saw his leg blown completely off except that inch. He said, "Oh, no, not my legs." I really distinctly remember the look on his face. Then he sort of went into semiconsciousness. He died on the way to the hospital. I had to walk up the trail to guard for the medivac to pick him up. And I remember praying to the Lord to let me see some VC - anybody - jump out on that trail.

From "Bloods" by Wallace Terry

Ignore everything I've written about Saigon

A leisurely coffee and then it's a quick and mindless 300ks to Saigon.

I try to tell myself not to use that name. "Saigon" is of the past; the new Vietnam is here, free of colonial influences.

So, Ho Chi Minh City it is.

But the new name sits haltingly on the tongue. Saigon slides off the palate like fine wine; it has resonance and nuance and speaks of tender and beautiful things. And, strangely - or, perhaps, understandably - the locals seem to feel the same. As I near the city, I come across a Saigon Hotel and, later, buy a Saigon beer. Even the buses have on their destination plates "Saigon" instead of HCMC.

As I ride through the increasingly congested traffic, I reflect on this place, its name, its past. Two things come to mind the moment I think of the word "Saigon", my brain's information retrieval system sorting the pure grain from the chaff: the first is the play "Miss Saigon" and the second, related to it in so many ways, those unforgettable images of the last helicopter leaving the American Embassy, rats deserting a sinking ship, barbarians at the door.

The tragic musical Miss Saigon tells the story of a Vietnamese bargirl abandoned by her GI lover as the Americans, tired now of a protracted and increasingly bloody war, cut their losses and pull out. The theme is all too familiar, a sad legacy of so many wars throughout time where soldiers leave behind them their unwanted children, some already born but most just taking human form in the warm wombs of local women. Many are the result of rape but most because the invaders are powerful and cash rich and the women weak and poor and need to feed their families.

The American soldiers left behind them some 26,000 pale-skinned, round-eyed children - so-called "children of dust" - who had to bear the consequent ostracism and stigma from a traditionally conservative society that looked with scorn upon women who had so obviously consorted with the enemy.

Later, the US government made an effort to bring some children of servicemen back to America. This was rather obviously called "Operation Babylift" but only about 3% of Ameriasian children were repatriated, the first flight crashing in the paddy fields outside Saigon and killing most of the children it was carrying...

And then the fall of Saigon, 29 April 1975. Who can forget the photographs of the last Huey UH-1 taking off from the roof of the US embassy, a desperate crowd of South Vietnamese who had broken through the iron gates and clambered up to the roof onto a small, square concrete structure just wide enough to accommodate the helicopter, holding out their arms in mute appeal while a US marine tried to hold them back so they didn't rush the Huey and bring it down. A desperate, defeated people trying to escape the advancing Viet Cong who in their bloodlust were meeting out summary justice in the streets to anyone they thought might have collaborated with the retreating enemy. Then, with a clatter of its rotors, the helicopter rose from the embassy roof, taking the last fourteen to safety. Thus ended what would be recognised as the largest helicopter evacuation in history.

On the aircraft carriers waiting offshore, so many aircraft were flying in that the decks became overwhelmed and sailors were pushing helicopters into the sea to make room for even more aircraft fleeing the advancing North Vietnamese troops. It had become a rout.

And so, for the Americans, the Vietnam War was over. Not so for the South Vietnamese who suffered years of persecution, vindictive retaliation, confiscation of property, deportation to re-education camps, loss of jobs as North Vietnamese officials were parachuted in to take control of key positions. All this despite the assurances from the north that all Vietnamese people were now part of the same country, united and free.

South Vietnamese began to flee, searching out a better life elsewhere, anywhere, and the Boat People became a daily part of our news just as today, in the latest diaspora, we view from the safety and warmth of our homes the images of desperate people clinging to overturned boats or huddled in small inflatable dinghies impossibly overloaded, their hands outstretched in the hope of rescue. Desperate times.

These things are in my thoughts as I make my way through gently wooded hills for most of the day until the city named after the saviour-like figure who orchestrated the defeat of America and changed humanity's attitude to war for generations: Ho Chi Minh.

It's not long before the wooded open spaces give way and the city begins to wrap me in its sweaty, noisy embrace. The frenetic urban sprawl of Saigon begins a full fifty kilometres from its centre, the snarl of traffic and drivers with suicidal intent, a writhing tangle of vehicles that curl and unfurl, joust and yield, the noise and the smell and the heat unbearable.

Somehow, more through luck than good judgement, I stumble upon backpackers' nirvana in the centre of Saigon, close to the river. I find a cheap guest house (my window, if you could call it that, opens onto a bare wall just inches from my face), strip off my sweaty clothes and wash them; get the road grime out of my pores.

Later, walking about the streets, I feel out of place; I don't belong here. There are too many white people about, mostly large people who carry their excess weight with a ponderous gait I have not seen for a while now. They are too clean, too young and earnest in their determination to have a good time. For the first time since entering Vietnam I am accosted by touts handing out restaurant menus, pamphlets extolling the joys of full-body massage, calling out to offer me a ride on a scooter, to buy some trashy souvenirs. And it's not just the young and the beautiful who flock to Vietnam on holiday; groups of old people are here too. I watch as they buy conical straw hats and walk about the streets looking silly.

I am too old to be part of the back packers' set; too young to be called old...

Eight pm. Ignore everything I've just written about Saigon.

A cold shower, the cleaner of my dirty shirts donned, two hours on my bed to revive the sagging bones and I emerge from my cocoon of sleep and step blinking and amazed into a fairyland of lights and buzz and atmosphere. Here the whole world has congregated to play, to forget about the realities of 9-5, the mortgage, and, just for a while, enter an adult playground. Bars and restaurants disgorge onto the streets a barrage of music, tables & chairs, people, touts handing out pamphlets and shouting, "Happy Hour - 2-for-1 drinks for the next hour..." so that only a narrow strip of road is still useable for its intended purpose and, into that, squeeze a thousand scooters, old women, seemingly just in from the country, selling from baskets slung from bamboo poles carried on one shoulder, fruit, plastic trinkets, Chinese fans, bracelets, pineapples peeled and cut into twirls, garish tourist junk. Women selling street food crouch on pavements in the entrances to dark alleys amongst the detritus of passing life, a single pot of noodles and meat bubbling over a gas cooker or a charcoal burner, plaintively calling out for custom in their high-pitched voices. Neon lights flash and pulsate, music and noise sucks me in, absorbs me and I am entranced. Now I can understand the siren call of the city, of the package-tour holiday, the fly-in, transport to the hotel, the bright entertainment of the night scene, buy a conical hat and bracelet to show your friends you've been there, the quick, see-everything-do-everything, all organised and done for you day trip to some pretty place where the locals don traditional garb and sing to you then back on the bus to the hotel and more night life...

I can understand that.

Me? I am tired and my clothes are dirty. Too dirty for any amount of washing to make respectable. My bike is dirt-covered - so much so that when I took it to the Honda dealership for a service as required by my contract, the mechanic in his white coat and gloves refused to touch it. Large motorcycle service centres in Vietnam are like operating theatres. You could eat off the workshop floor; the mechanics wear white, open-necked shirts and white gloves.

But, somehow, dirt and sweat and hassle thrown in, I wouldn't exchange what I do; it feels, somehow, more real.

I walk in a daze along transformed streets; beautiful girls in tight hot-pants invite me to enter their premises for a massage; I smile at them and shake my head. One takes my hand and hugs me, her eyes and her smile making me believe, for a brief moment, that I am special. I squeeze her hand and tell her no, thank you, not tonight. They are sweet girls. I shake my head at a hundred restaurant menus thrust into my face, happy-hour deals. Not tonight, thank you. No thank you. Sorry, no thank you. No, no massage, thank you...

The young and the beautiful are out to play. I am not one of them. In every bar, back-packers gather and chat. You can't miss them: early twenties, displaying their long, tanned limbs and faces open to possibilities, nursing beers, all speaking English in accents that reveal their origins, English often better spoken than many who inhabit our mother-tongue isles; strong, independent young people on the cusp of adulthood, setting out on this grand adventure of life, discovering the world before the world ties them down and wears them out and rubs the adventure out of them.

This is how it ought to be. This is what growing up into responsible adulthood is all about. I look into their earnest happy faces as I navigate my way through the pavement chaos and I am content.

Later I pause at some faceless bar and sip at a beer. At a table next to mine an old man - about my age, I suppose - sits alongside a pretty young Vietnamese girl-woman who clings to his liver-spotted arm assuring him with her lying eyes that he is young and virile again...

Eight am. Disregard everything I've just written about Saigon.

It doesn't exist.

It's a fallacy; a dream. It's smoke and mirrors; a false reality...

I walk out of my clammy, anonymous room (with open window looking out onto a bare brick wall), and step onto the street.

It's gone.

Midnight has struck and the ugly sisters still rule the house.

I stare, disbelieving, at a street stripped of its bright tinsel, ragged and bare at the edges.

The emperor is, indeed, naked.

A lone woman wearing a dirty, shapeless dress sweeps last night's filth from the street and pavement into the gutter where she makes neat piles that steam and stink in the heat. Around her the traffic writhes and snarls.

The bright lights and enchantment of the night before has reverted to empty cigarette packets and discarded beer cans, to the smells of foetid matter and blocked drains. Old women still crouch in the gutters over their meagre fare, their simmering pots and baskets of food, the small, bright plastic chairs set out, backs to alley walls. It's as if they have never left, that the street has become their home. The cycle of supplying food to passers-by so that they themselves can eat has become the defining fact of their lives. They have nothing of the quaint about them in the harsh light of day; in them I see only the aching despair of hungry rural people who gravitate to the cities of the world in a desperate attempt to make some kind of tenuous living. The bustle and the noise is still here, but not the lights. It was the lights that transformed something inherently ugly into a wonderland, a magical playground, for just a few hours.

I walk about, already sweaty, and look for a Honda service centre. The beautiful people and the young at heart with their bright eyes and tanned skin have emerged from their sleep and are clustered about Internet cafes and backpacker hostels, waiting for the mini-bus to take them to whatever attraction is on offer today.

Back at my hostel I grab my soap and walk into the shower. Two young women, torsos wrapped in white towels, their smooth, lithe backs tanned and freshly washed, stand at the basins.

"Whoah!" I cry, starting to back out. "Is this a unisex thing or is there a..."

"Unisex," the pretty reflections in the mirror say, laughing their white teeth at me.

* * * * *

When I had just got into my squad, Tango squad, I said, "Anybody here from D.C.?"

There was one brother, Richard Streeter, from D.C., who I used to go with his wife in high school. I mean they weren't married when I was in high school.

Then this white brother said, "Say, hey, I'm from D.C."

I said, "Okay. Just as soon as I set up we'll get together."

He began to set up, too. He went down to the water hole to fill up his canteen. On his way back, he stepped on a 500-lb bomb that was laid in a tank track.

You don't walk in no tank tracks, because that's where the bombs are usually. Charlie would use the rationale that most tanks would follow their tracks, and they would booby-trap tank tracks.

We didn't see that white brother anymore. All we saw was a big crater, maybe six feet deep. And some remains. You know, guts and stuff. And the dirt had just enveloped the stuff. It looked like batter on fish and batter on chicken pieces. His body looked like that.

From "Bloods" by Wallace Terry

A girl's gotta make a living

By mid-afternoon on my second day in Saigon, I am feeling again the call of the open road. There are just so many times I can say No, thank you - politely and with a smile - to old, bent women who try to sell me gaudy knick-knacks or plastic Chinese fans or cigarettes; or men who try to sell me kitsch paintings of stylised rural Vietnamese scenes or attractive young women offering menus or massages. I know they are just trying to earn an honest buck, so being rude or showing frustration is an unnecessary indulgence that the haves are able to wield over the have-nots of this world. But, as I say, there are just so many times I can smile and say no; only so much techno-beat coming from themed bars I can take before I begin to lose the will to live.

This is not Vietnam. This is an ersatz impression of the Vietnam those who run the tourist industry want to sell to tourists. It's a false construct. I need to escape its glossy veneer and its constant demands on my attention. So, seeing a narrow alleyway just off the main tourist street, I slip inside and, in a moment, it's gone. Behind the facade, real life is being lived by real people in the rabbit warren of dark alleys, barely an arm's length wide, that link the main streets. Sunlight is barely able to penetrate from the pale sliver of sky some 50-ft up between concrete walls that seem to lean inwards as they rise through a tangle of electric wires and telephone cables and limp strings of washing hung up to dry.

I make my way deeper into the maze of narrow, dark passageways, taking turns at random, past and between old men dozing on tatty chairs as if the alleyway is the porch outside their front door; I step over children's toys and around the children playing with them; I pass women preparing food on the alley floor, crouched over plastic bowls, a man repairing his scooter, a young girl washing clothes in a bucket. I feel out of place here too; I am intruding into their private space. My world ought to be out on the bright street, spending money and doing what tourists do.

But I don't feel at home there either.

When does attempting to reach, however briefly, into the real lives of people in a foreign land turn into voyeurism?

I come across a middle-aged woman washing clothes; she crouches flat-footed and with splayed knees over a plastic bucket in the middle of the alley. Feeling that I am about to cross my own self-imposed boundary, that I am straying too closely into her personal space, I pause and am about to turn back but she looks up at me and waves me on with wet hands. I inch past her, back against the wall, and continue down the alley to emerge much later, blinking and disorientated, onto the busy street with its bright sunlight and its noise and the insistent voices tugging at the corners of my mind.

A sense of calmness has come upon me from walking through the hidden lives of ordinary folk and I set off, further afield, away from tourist land. And within 300 metres I have entered a different world. The tourists have gone. It is as if they have been corralled into a small space where touristy things happen, like a carefully prepared stage set with extras in traditional dress selling trinkets and offering services aimed at those who fly in, see the sights and fly home again clutching their *I Love Saigon* T-shirt while normal Vietnamese life goes on just a few streets away. I find I am walking along a pavement crowded with sellers of fruit and vegetables, dried fish, sacks of grain; old women crouch over their wares and watch me as I pass; a toothless old man greets me - not the officious greeting of the tout, the false bonhomie of the seeker after money - just a genuine greeting to a stranger walking past. Next to the vegetable sellers, a small, garage-sized room houses a workshop full of lathes and presses and drilling machines. I pause and watch as a thin man with greasy hands, stripped to the waist because of the heat, his dark olive skin glistening with sweat, cuts fine ribbons of waste from a piece of metal clamped in the jaws of a lathe. On a street corner a young man calls to me and invites me to say hello to his small child who sits in a walking ring and stares at me with black eyes. She has a square head covered with short hair. A little further on thin-faced mechanics pull out the innards of scooter engines in small workshops opening out onto the pavement; another man works on the wiring of a Harley rat-bike. I pause to watch.

Old men sit in the sun, the wisdom of their years deeply etched into their bewiskered faces. Then there are cell-like rooms just off the street where waste is being sorted for re-cycling. Women wearing sacking over-clothes push trolleys laden with flattened cardboard boxes down the street. One, as she passes, points at me and speaks earnestly to me in Vietnamese. I don't understand but she persists. Eventually I realise she is warning not to carry my mobile phone in my hand, to put it away safely in my pocket. I thank her and she continues on her way, pushing her heavy load.

A crowd of men and women stand about on the pavement looking with hopeful eyes at a shop window where the latest lottery results are being posted. To one side, three young men, crouched on their hams, play cards, the concrete pavement their table.

And, strangely, in amongst the smells and the dust, the discarded vegetable skins, the ragged people who are deemed ugly by the standards of our Western world, I feel happy, at peace. I pause and drink a cup of ice coffee for which I pay 15,000D instead of the usual 52,000 I've just paid for a bottle of Coke in the tourist area.

After a gentle, quiet hour, I turn back. And then, all too soon, it starts again: "Hey, mister, you want cigarettes? Two-for-one Happy Hour? Nice fan? You want massage...?"

Back at the hostel, I meet San, a Londoner. He is a sad young man, confused and hurting. At 29, he still lives at home with a father who believes, he tells me, that the husband - the father, the *man* - is king, one who ought to be obeyed. His father doesn't ask or talk, he instructs and expects to be obeyed. And that is how he treats his wife, the young man's mother.

I probe - and his story is interesting. I'll tell it in his own words: *"During the American War, my parents lived in North Vietnam. But we were originally from China. My parents left China and moved to Vietnam to escape the shit that was happening there. Then the war was won. The Communists won. But the Communists fucked up the country. China lied. Ho Chi Minh deceived us. In 1979 China invaded Vietnam and so did Cambodia. The VC pushed them back. They were good soldiers. They'd had ten years' experience fighting the Americans. But because China invaded, all people of Chinese extraction living in Vietnam were looked at with suspicion. My parents had to get out. They left everything, lost everything. First they went to Hong Kong and then, after a few years, to the UK. My parents couldn't speak English, but my father got a job as a tailor, making clothes at £2.50 an hour. He worked day and night, as all Chinese do. And he saved. And he watched everything that was going on in the factory. And when he'd learned everything he needed, he left and started his own factory. He made a lot of money. But he treated us and my mother badly because he was the man, he was the one with the money. Mao Zedong and Ho Chi Minh believed in dictatorship, autocracy, even though they claimed to be Communist. They were the leaders and everyone had to do what they said. And fathers, Chinese fathers, learned it from them."*

"You need to get away," I tell him. "Live your own life..."

He doesn't say anything, just hangs his head, frowning.

Later, when darkness has descended once again across the streets of Saigon and the fairy lights have been turned on, I meet a one-eyed woman with a limp who has appropriated twenty metres of an alley as her business premises. She stakes her claim by setting out small plastic chairs, 12-inches high, along both sides of the graffiti-covered walls and defends it aggressively when any other hawker dares approach. So we sit, about forty of us, backs to a ratty brick wall, feet pressed against a filthy alley surface, so narrow that only scooters can pass between us, and we consume ready-made fruit smoothies such as I have never experienced before. The atmosphere is, under the concealing darkness and occasional dim electric bulb, somehow enchanting.

I allow myself just a moment to see it as it really is: a dirty, litter-filled alley upon whose rutted surface we are sitting, noisy scooters screaming by just inches from our feet...

But in the enchantment of the evening light, it has become a fairy-tale world again.

As the evening turns to night, I pause to chat with one of the delightful young ladies offering the delights of a massage. She presses a pamphlet into my hand, her small hands tugging at my arm. The cost of a head and shoulders massage is a pittance so, purely in the interest of experience, I agree after she points out a 20% discount for day-time massages. There is a kind of desperation in her eyes.

I smile at her and nod my head and she tucks my arm into the crook of her elbow, claiming me. She leads me down a side alley, dark and just a little threatening, and into a doorway. I wonder whether I am setting myself up to be mugged; expect to be confronted by a group of hard-eyed men with knives who demand money. The young lass leads me, still clutching my arm, into a dimly-lit room. A grumpy-looking older woman jabs a finger at the 12-4pm restriction for the 20% discount but my young lass remonstrates. I can't understand but imagine her pleading, "Gimme me a break, man! I've been out on the street for hours. My feet hurt. A girl's gotta make a living..."

We agree on the reduced fee and the grumpy woman insists on payment in advance. I pay - about £2.00 - certain that I'm about to be scammed. My young lass again takes me by the arm and leads me up a narrow stairway. I bump my head on a low overhang but she has foreseen this and has placed her hand on top of my head. It seems to have hurt her. She has a tattoo of a flower on her upper thigh.

Once upstairs she leads me into a darkened room with four massage tables roughly separated from each other by sheets hung from the ceiling. She asks me to lie down on my back and rubs my neck and shoulders with coconut oil; the pungent odour surrounds me with its heady perfume. For the next half hour, she stands behind me and attempts to rearrange my scalp, face, neck and shoulders with strong, insistent fingers.

She has no English so I don't attempt to communicate with her, although I so want to ask about her life, her family, her plans for the future. Instead, I close my eyes and relax.

Nothing untoward happens. I am not assaulted by accomplices with scars who barge into the room and demand money. She does not suggest other services for an additional fee; her manner is never coquettish. Just a pretty, sweet kid trying to make her way in a harsh world.

I realise that the grumpy woman downstairs probably takes most of the money; that this young girl will be working on commission, which might explain the desperation in her eyes and the offer of an unauthorised discount.

When she is finished she doesn't stand expectantly waiting for a tip. Once again she takes me by the arm and is about to lead me down the stairs, past the grumpy woman and out onto the street where she will again take her stand late into the night, handing out pamphlets with hope in her eyes to passers-by who brush past without a glance, without a look that might confer upon her the dignity of recognition.

I ask her to wait, take out my wallet and press into her hand a note equal to what I had originally paid.

"For you," I tell her.

She smiles at me and leads me down the stairs.

Later in the evening, I pass her again in the street, still standing where I left her, pamphlets held out towards tourists who brush by, uninterested.

And there passes between us a glance of mutual recognition and she smiles...

* * * * *

One time, the VC we found in the village we was going to take back, because we found him with a .50-caliber machine gun - an antiaircraft-type gun - and a lot of ammo. We felt that this man knows something.

This brother and the squad leader, a white dude, for some reason they felt they could interrogate this man. This man wasn't speaking any English. They did not speak any Vietnamese. I could not understand that at all. We push him into a chopper and take him high up. They hollerin', "Where you come from? How many you?" And they callin' him everything - Dink, Gook. Motherfucker. He couldn't say anything. He was scared.

The next thing I know, the man was out of the helicopter.

I turned round and asked the folks what happened to him.

They told me he jumped out.

I said, "Naw, man. The man ain't jumped out."

The brother said, "Yes, he did. He one of those tough VC."

I didn't believe it. The brother was lying to me, really.

I turned round and the man was gone. I didn't actually see him pushed, but he was gone. It took a long time for me to believe it. I just kept looking where he sat at. And I couldn't deal with it.

From "Bloods" by Wallace Terry

Song to make tourists happy

The next day I find myself sitting on a comfortable seat in an air-conditioned bus heading south towards the Mekong Delta. Our tour guide, Bimh, makes silly jokes about the driver not having a licence. His accent is broad and I struggle to make out what he says. He breaks off intermittently to sing cheesy songs in Vietnamese and English and gets for his efforts a brief and derisory applause from those of us trapped in the bus...

I have, for a brief time, betrayed my status as traveller and become a tourist. For this weakness I am forced to submit to the corny jokes and karaoke singing of our tour guide and the promise of being taught a Vietnamese song later in the day.

Can't wait.

We leave the urban sprawl of Saigon and travel fast through a flat land greened with rice paddies. Inside it is hot and airless. After two hours, the bus pulls over. We are told by our ever-ebullient guide that we have twenty minutes to visit a Buddhist monastery. Outside, a smooth white statue of the Buddha, thirty foot high, with his pendulous ear lobes and comfortable stomach, presents his happy face to the land. The heat is oppressive. We walk past the inevitable stands selling cheap souvenirs, sunglasses and hats into the cool, deep gloom of the monastery. The musty smell of age surrounds me like a presence.

I separate myself from the group and look for hidden corners, passages and rooms where visitors are not expected to go. I don't want to see what has been prepared for the eyes of tourists, polished and brightly-coloured, on display with flashing coloured lights and bowls of fruit; I want to see underneath the facade.

The monastery is very old, its wooden beams heavy and gnarled. There is a peace here, a coolness in the shaded interior with faded Chinese-style frescos on the walls; dust-covered wooden trestle tables and benches, the heavy planks, hand-cut and joined, stand on wooden floors stained dark with the tread of many feet. The very air carries within itself the whispers of monks whose bare feet trod these planks hundreds of years ago, before the French, before Catholicism, long before the persecution of the Buddhist majority by the pro-Catholic president Ngo Dinh Diem and the ritual self-immolation of 73-year-old monk Thich Quang Duc whose fiercely burning body stood in stark contrast to the peace on his face as he sat, cross-legged, hands resting in his lap, closed eyes looking inward, head proudly raised as the flames peeled the flesh from his bones.

As I stand in the shadows trying to catch the dry whispers of long-gone monks, an old woman shuffles past me and stands in front of a dusty shrine that has about it the patina of age. She is oblivious of me, the onlooker, the voyeur, her eyes focused on the Buddha, hands pressed together in an attitude of prayer. I watch her wrinkled lips move, mouthing silent words from the heart's core. She bows at the waist three times, stares immovable for a long time and then, as silently as she has entered, she leaves, making her way through a crowd of tourists *click-clicking* with their cameras, taking selfies and posing for friends in front of joss-stick-wreathed shrines. The bent old lady seems not to notice them; absorbed still in her private moment of devotion, she makes her way out the door and into the sun.

"*Quick-quick!*" the smiling Bimh cries, clapping his hands and pointing to his watch. The bus is ready, engine running. Our visit to the monastery is over.

As soon as we are back on the road, the barely intelligible Bimh beams at us and rattles off a five-minute potted history of Buddhism. I remember something about someone waking up with something in her stomach - seven bulls? - and then going about preaching and looking up and down and the karma. Yes, karma, I know about that. He then goes on to tell us that, in Buddhism, if you do good you have a long life and are healthy and if you do bad you die early and are unhealthy.

Buddhist temple and lecture on Buddhism - tick.

Karma... Funny, I know a lot of absolute shits who have lived a very long time and some good people who died young. Explain, please.

I don't want to sound flippant; I'm not sneering at an old and gracious religion here - just the package tour experience, the Quick-quick... Oooh, look at the statue of Buddha (pose... selfie)... quick-quick, back on the bus... right, this is what Buddhism is all about, now, another song?

Then the great Mekong River, slow moving and brown. We disembark from the bus and are led through a jostle of tourists onto our boat. Heavily laden sampans nudge their way through flotillas of tourist boats as we make our way to an island in the middle of the river. Old ladies teeter on the edge as the rocking boat nudges a concrete pier. We are led through the ubiquitous tourist tat stands and sit down on plastic chairs while - yes, it really is happening and I steel myself for the cliche - a group of five women with vacant eyes sing a bored rendition of a traditional song. A few in our party clap their hands ironically. The ladies in colourful dresses do not respond to the desultory applause. They have one more song to sing and, with expressionless faces, they intone *If you're happy and you know it clap your hands* before moving across the way to yet another tourist group who have shuffled in under the fussy direction of their guide.

I joke not.

Local culture, women in traditional dress sing traditional song and song to make tourists happy - tick.

A brief hiatus that Bimh fills by singing another song, holding an imaginary microphone to his lips. I have a strange feeling that he believes we think he's good.

This whole experience is bloody horrible.

We are led to a wooden jetty where a gaggle of sampans awaits us. I step into one with a few other tourists, then a middle-aged Vietnamese woman with thin arms and wearing a conical hat paddles us along a narrow, muddy channel which would be beautiful were we not jostled by thirty other tourist-filled sampans being paddled along the same narrow channel through the mangroves as clogged as the streets of Saigon are with scooters. Bimh is in my sampan and he offers me a conical hat, holds out his hand for my camera and says, "One dollar."

I shake my head.

Photo of tourist wearing silly hat while being paddled in sampan - cross.

We climb out of our sampans and walk a short way (past trestle tables selling conical hats, dark glasses and plastic Buddhas) where we are offered the opportunity of draping a bored python around our necks while photographs are taken.

Tourist with python around neck - photo opportunity - tick.

Back onto the large sampan, Bimh sings to us again above the noise of the engine, "Wherever you go, whatever you do, I'll be right here waiting for you." He grins and offers for us to stand on the prow of the boat and do a Gwyneth Paltrow while he takes a photograph. No takers.

Fortunately the trip is a short one or I might have had to push him over the side.

But the roughly-built sampans made of heavy planking and with the traditional eyes painted on the prow, single-cylinder engine hammering its vibration through the hull, the boat nosing its way through the muddy Mekong waters between banks thick with tall fern and mangrove trees is atmospheric and strangely authentic despite the camera-toting tourists.

And as I sit at a table with a clean cloth under a shady woven cane roof, fans wafting cooling air over me, a waiter places a pre-prepared meal in front of me, another offers me a cold beer and I think, yes, despite my cynicism, despite the cliched, tinsel falseness of this whole experience, I have seen a beautiful old Buddhist monastery full of history and hidden stories; I have sat in a traditionally made sampan on the Mekong River; I'm clean and refreshed and cool; I haven't had to sit in the heat on the roadside and eat a few pieces of fruit for my lunch because of the hassle of trying to find something palatable and not noodle-based and, tonight, my place of sleeping has already been chosen for me, a cold beer and a meal awaits, and, tomorrow, someone will pick me up and take me back onto the river to see the floating market, something that for a long time I have wanted to experience and I won't have had to hunt around on my bike for a place to stay or for someone to take me onto the river at the crack of dawn, negotiate a price, struggle with the language... It's all been done for me - in a rather cheesy way, granted, but it's been relaxing and fun. On the way, I've met and chatted with a group of Iranian Kurds and discussed the history of the Kurdish people and their future prospects of obtaining a unified state; a young English man with his Czech wife. On my bike I would have had only myself for company and that can get pretty lonely at times.

Yes, I can understand the attraction of these short package tours although, like my time in Saigon, just a tiny slice is sufficient for me. And I would trade it all for a brief time spent with the man beating aluminium rims into circles and the pieces of apple his retarded son offered me with his sweet smile.

Back to the bus. Darkness is setting in. As we pass through a junction there is a sickening crash. I peer out the bus window. On the road are three bodies and scattered bits of scooter.

We drive around them. I crane my neck to look out the back window of the bus and see two youngsters, a boy and a girl, drag themselves to their feet amongst the wreckage of their bikes. The third lies ominously still.

We leave the smashed bikes and the crumpled body for someone else to care for. After all, that's reality; we're just tourists and we haven't come here for that.

A short while later the bus stops and eight of us get out and are led by a little girl across a flat, watery land cut by levees; tracks and paths and roads have been raised above the level of the water which surrounds us on every side, a land of rivers and estuaries and houses on stilts. Boats replace cars and the rivers have become highways. On the levees banana, papaya and coconut palms grow; down below, rice paddies paint the land green.

The rest of the tour group on the bus have opted to spend the night in a hotel; our small band - an English guy married to a girl from the Czech Republic; an Albanian-born chef, now living in Italy, travelling with a young Australian girl; an itinerant Auzzie - now on his 65th country, he informs us with a certain degree of pride; two Greeks and me, a South African-born Brit - will be staying with a Vietnamese family.

We are allocated thatch-roofed rooms raised above the level of the water and I unpack. Later a child calls us to the dining room where we are fed. We drink cold beers and solve the problems of the world until late.

At midnight I retire, leaving Anthony, the Pom, and Michael, the Auzzie, friends now until the next rugby match rekindles old rivalries, attempting to drink the fridge dry in a manner characteristic of their breed - a practice, fortunately, I have never felt the need to cultivate.

* * * * *

One night we set up an L-shaped ambush at this crossing outside this village. Charlie is supposed to come down this street. All of a sudden GIs - I guess about 15 of us - are taking off guns, hats, shirts, pants, everything. This place is just loaded with black ants, and they would sting. Man, those ants burnt our behinds up. It was like we were standing in hot water.

We were making so much noise when somebody said, "Here comes Charlie."

I'm thinking, Well, damn, you know they have to know where we are. They had to hear us.

But they just came walking right on up the trail. I still can't understand this. We sprung the doggone ambush in our undershorts, supposedly killed four of them. And we don't have no bodies. Haven't got a damn thing to show for it. You can go out there and see where there was some blood.

I don't know where these guys go when you kill 'em. It's just that they just vanish. Somewhere. I don't know. Maybe the twilight zone.

From "Bloods" by Wallace Terry

The cocks don't feel up to performing for us today

Cocks crow me awake. It's still dark and blessedly cool. Michael, who shares my room, is still asleep. As the sun rises, the others, bleary-eyed, rouse themselves and drink strong coffee.

Later, our host, infant son tucked under one arm, leads us along a palm-lined path next to the river. Dogs bark at us as we pass. The child stares about him with bright eyes, his black hair standing straight up from his head.

The river, when we reach it, is slow and muddy; mangrove roots pencil the air through thick, yellow-brown mud; smoke from early-morning fires hazes the air.

We climb onto our boat, a large fibreglass thing that lacks the romance of a traditional wooden sampan paddled by a wizened old man I had hoped for. Our pilot starts up the engine, lowers the long propeller shaft into the water, and we set off through a maze of dirty brown channels full of small floating islands of Kariba weed that swirl and tip as our wash catches them. On the riverbank, stilted houses settle in the mud; the barnacles growing on their wooden piles reveal the high tide line.

We pass a man standing chest-deep in the river resetting a broken wooden pile while a woman holds it in place from the balcony above. Netting to catch adventurous children covers the overhanging balconies where washing is hung out to dry; exposed river banks glisten mud-wet in the early light. We look into the back doors of passing homes, the small balcony back yards of the river-dwellers, and watch the normality of their lives as we pass by: a child flings dust sweepings into the water; a man feeds pigeons in a hutch; ferns grow in pots amongst brightly-coloured washing; standing up to his waist in the water, a man washes his naked body that glistens in the early morning sunlight.

The tide is low; the mangrove pneumatophores stand a foot above the mud as if stretching for air. Under the piles supporting their homes, children scrabble about and play in the riverbank shallows; a young woman sets fish traps in the mud.

The sun is up and suddenly it is hot. A sampan approaches rapidly and manoeuvres itself against our hull; a shrill-voiced woman hooks a rope onto a car-tyre buffer and offers us iced coffee; another sampan appears, attaches itself to our moving hull, and a woman wearing a conical hat leans into a window and tries to sell coconut juice.

Moored in the centre of the river are the bigger boats, the water-borne distribution warehouses of the delta. The water bustles with commerce. A little boy, standing on a boat deck piled high with bananas, calls out, "One dollar, one dollar..." Clumps of weed and foliage cling to mooring ropes as the tide begins to turn, pulling them towards the sea. Pineapples, coconuts, cartons of bananas, watermelons are thrown from a loaded boat to a man who stands high on a levee. Behind him a street stall offers wares to passing motorists.

While we wait to be transferred to yet another boat, a middle-aged Australian man with a young Vietnamese woman companion engages me in conversation. "We opted for the hotel last night," he tells me, almost conspiratorially. Then, with his mouth twisted into a sneer, he adds, "In the old days home stay could mean a hut in a rice paddy with a local family - no English, just living like the peasants..." and I look at him.

He's serious.

"I'd have loved that," I say and he turns away.

Somehow, I think he's missed the point...

Would I do the package tour thing again?

Yes. But I'd go, knowing that it's little more than a neat slice of fabricated life placed on a microscope slide for us to gawk at. Parts of the experience are educational. I learned today, for example, how rice noodles are made; I watched the fire that heats the metal plate on which the rice slurry is poured fuelled by the discarded husks of the rice grains. Good. I accept the stalls of tourist tat that one is required to walk past before each staged exhibit as an understandable distraction. Some of what we look at as we ride click-clicking by is real life being led by real people; some of these people interact with us, use us as a resource selling water and cool drinks, iced coffee and trinkets as we pass; most go on with their lives, as oblivious of us as the animals in a game reserve become, inured by a life-time of tourist-carrying 4X4s that drive past them each day until they can live and sleep, kill and fornicate as we watch them from the safety of our vehicles.

It's a trade-off in the end. Not everyone can be an explorer. Time and money, age and inclination restricts us, so this brief peer onto the staged slice of life that has been prepared and performed for us is all some of us can get. I count my blessings that I've been able to delve a little deeper. To each his own - but so long as we understand that it is, in many ways, nothing more than a construct.

So we ride bicycles along a narrow dirt track around a large island in the delta, the path shaded by an exuberant growth of bamboo, coconut palm and banana trees; breadfruit, like small green armadillos, hang from the bowls of trees; mud and water ooze to fill any depression deeper than a foot; children play bright-skinned in the turgid water and bare-necked fowls run off the path as we pass; a fig tree spreads its branches, a net of woven limbs pock-marking the soil with patches of light.

Promised the spectacle of watching a pair of cocks rip each other to death in an orgy of bloody feathers, we are informed that the cocks don't feel up to performing for us today, thank you. Another con. My Australian friend tells me he feels like he's been promised a beer and given a glass of water.

Unpainted, flat-bottomed boats, some rotted through, are drawn up onto the mud, awaiting the tide.

Iron barges, so laden their gunnels are awash, butt their way up river. Later we come across a large boat, mired in a mud-bound tributary, making laborious and halting progress by using the digger loaded on its deck as a mechanical arm, scooping it through the mud a few metres at a time...

* * * * *

I still dream about Vietnam.

In one dream, everybody has nine lives. I've walked in front of machine guns that didn't go off. When they pulled the trigger, the trigger jammed. I've seen situations where I got shot at, and the round curved and hit the corner. I'd see that if I'd not made that one step, I would not be here. I think about the time when a rocket-propelled grenade hit me in the back, and it didn't go off. We were in a clear area and got hit by an enemy force. The RPG hit me. It didn't go off. Didn't explode. We kept walking and five of us got hit. I got frags in the lower back and right part of the buttocks. I didn't want to go back to the hospital ship, so I just created the impression that I could handle it. But the stuff wouldn't stop bleeding, and they had to pull the frags out. There was this doctor at Quang Tri, Dr Mitchell, who was from Boston, a super guy. He painted a smile on my rear end. He cut a straight wound into a curve with stitches across so it looks as if I'm smiling. When I drop my trousers, there's a big smile.

From "Bloods" by Wallace Terry

A thoroughfare of sampans - looking for blank spaces on the map

My last night in Saigon. I check into my hostel, shower and then, later, I find, by happy accident, an oasis of calm run by a balding, overweight Pom who oversees his establishment with a gentle benevolence punctuated by smiling profanities. One wall of his eatery is filled with shelves of paperbacks (for sale or trade) and boxed games that patrons can borrow and play in an aura of quiet retreat, a refuge from the heat and the noise and the insistent demands on your attention just metres from his door.

He suggests a beer; I browse and purchase a book. At the table next to me a young couple play Scrabble and, just outside the door, four middle-aged Englishmen with paunches and wearing vests, smoke, drink beer and talk football.

While drinking my beer, a slight man in his early forties appears at my elbow and asks if he can share my table. He tells me he has recently lost his wife of three years to an aggressive form of cancer and he is trying to get his life back. His name is Jimmy and he's doing a cycle tour with an organised group. He tears up as he tells me about his wife, the emotion still raw and close to the surface.

Later, while perusing my phone, I happen upon my old school website and come across a list of Old Boys who have passed away. The list is long and I am shocked to note just how many of them were classmates of mine.

Am I, I wonder, reaching that stage of life when one begins to check the weekly obituary pages in the newspaper to see who else has cashed in their chips, counting those who are left and wondering...

Carpe diem, man, *carpe diem...*

I find a pub with sport on the big screen and watch Wales beat Italy. Rugby, of course. Set my alarm for four to watch the England game but when I get there, bleary-eyed, it's all over. They had the wrong time on the board outside. I go back to bed.

Sleep until ten - two hours late - and then pick up my trusty bike that has been waiting for the past two days. Load up and am on my way in thirty minutes. So good to have a bike between my legs again. If offered the choice of a hot wind breathing against my bare forearms or an air-conditioned seat in a bus, I'd take the hot wind.

I head South out of the city for fifty kilometres then, at Tan An, turn West to follow a small road that seems to have been drawn on the map with a ruler across a flat, watery land for 150ks. I'm aiming for a blank space called "Plain of Reeds". Why? Because it sounds interesting, I suppose. The thin, straight road traverses more blank spaces on the map, intersected only by what look like man-made water channels or canals. The intention is to put a little distance between people and me - just for a while.

I ride across a flat land, hot and humid, foetid with life. Water is the natural element here with soil and the spawning growth upon it an afterthought. Rivers and their tributaries meander their way through while canals, ruler-straight, cut liquid grids across the land. Look on a map and the whole vastness of this delta is spider-webbed with blue lines. A thoroughfare of sampans.

Rice-paddies chop the land into neat squares; sunlight glints off the still surface water as I ride past, high on the raised levees. I pass through a centre of milling where trucks piled high with sacks of newly harvested rice line up on the roadside, waiting their turn to disgorge their loads down grid-covered chutes. Moored in wide channels alongside, large wooden boats take away the dry rice husks, their carrying capacity increased by long bamboo poles, cloth-covered, like sails protruding from both sides. Because the inland waters are slow-flowing and still, sampans can be loaded until their gunnels are awash. At times I pause and watch large boats so laden they seem to be in the process of sinking - just the stern, prow and a slightly raised lip around the hold are above water - nosing their way along wide canals, slow-flowing with their heavy load of silt. Any restless sea would sink them.

In the smaller rivers and creeks, ducks wallow in brown water so thick with mud it doesn't flow, it oozes. Ducks, thousands of them, tens of thousands, turn muddy banks white. And scooped out of the soil, deep water-filled basins mark the presence of fish farms.

Soon I am lost, bearing in mind that the word "lost" has meaning only when one has a definite destination. The network of small tracks, some too narrow for a car, lead me into the web of this flat land, alongside water-hyacinth-clogged canals crossed by little hump-backed bridges made from concrete and precarious looking wooden structures that wobble and vibrate as I cross. Banana leaves hang over the track and brush my face as I pass; palms grow tall, lining the banks, their roots in the water.

I come across an army barracks, show my map to a group of bored-looking soldiers resting in the shade of a veranda and they tell me I must go back and find my way around. My map shows a small track directly through here but obviously the army has decided to build a re-supply base across it. I turn and take ever-diminishing roads and paths alongside narrow waterways, trying to make progress to the west.

At last I stumble upon a wider road and begin to make progress. The small patches of subsistence farming, the fishponds and duck farms, give way to vast cultivated fields of rice. From horizon to horizon the whole world is a pale, flat green cut through with raised, earthen levees. In some places, young gum trees have been planted along the roadside and the air is perfumed with eucalyptus. Occasionally the smooth carpet of green is interrupted by bright flashes of intense red where ripe chillies have been laid out on strips of cloth to dry.

The last twenty kilometres into An Long, a small village on the banks of the Mekong, the road is narrow and busy with life. Other than the ubiquitous scooters, I have to make my careful way around children playing, bone-thin men pushing loaded barrows, and chickens who seem to believe that food is more abundant on the road surface itself rather than in the thick grass on either side. As usual in Vietnam, the road seems to be a natural extension of the front parlour of houses, more so here because living space has been constricted by the flooded land. Consequently, houses are built with their chins resting on the levee edge, their back sections extending over the water and propped up by wooden piles. The houses, and life lived in them, is so close to the road that the smells of evening meals being prepared come clearly to me through the air as I pass.

The sun sets low on the horizon and, as I am riding due west, the dust in the air and the smoke from cooking fires turn the sky a deep orange. Eventually I reach the Mekong River and pause to gaze across its wide, slow-flowing expanse. This river rises in the high Tibetan Plateau and flows for 4,350 kilometres through China, Myanmar, Laos, Thailand and Cambodia before entering Vietnam in the extreme southwest. It drains an area of 795,000 square kilometres and deposits approximately 457 cubic *kilometres* of water into the South China Sea annually. Each year, after the monsoon rains, severe disruption to life and property is caused as the Mekong overflows its banks and floods vast tracts of land in the Delta; but, at the same time, mud that has been carried for so many thousands of kilometres is deposited, making this one of the most fertile areas in the world, home to some twenty million Vietnamese.

Finding no immediate way to cross and the sun now having set, I am faced with a choice: turn right towards Cambodia or left towards the southern delta region and, eventually, the sea.

I make my way down a small alley between houses right to the riverbank. There I pause again, look out at the large, sea-going ships and sampans moored in the river or nudging their slow way upstream. As I gaze across its still surface, I understand a little more the difficulty of attempting to control this vast inter-webbed net of inland waterways during the Vietnam/American War. These rivers and canals made transporting soldiers and equipment relatively easy for the North Vietnamese who were infiltrating this region and developing networks of resistance to the American occupation. And the American patrol boats became easy targets to ambush from hidden positions on the banks, so much so that they too were targeted for defoliation using Agent Orange.

As the fading light silvers the river, I can almost hear the slow beat of the USS San Pablo making its slow way up river, Steve McQueen and his Chinese mechanic, grease-stained down in the engine room, Candace Bergman looking serene in the fading light...

And I know it was the Yangtse River and not the Mekong, China and not Vietnam, 1926 and not 1968 - but somehow as the evening calm settles on the land and the water, it seems about right.

There being nowhere to stay in An Long, I continue south and follow the river towards the next large town, Cao Lanh. Hot, sweaty and very tired, I stumble upon a small but pleasant hotel about ten ks out of town.

Tomorrow I begin my long, slow way back to Hanoi.

* * * * *

The first one I killed really got to me. I guess it was his size. Big guy. Big, broad chest. Stocky legs. He was so big I thought he was Chinese. I still think he was Chinese.

We were on this trail near the Ashau Valley. I saw him and hit the ground and came up swinging like Starsky and Hutch. I shot him with a .45, and I got him pretty good.

He had an AK47. He was still holding it. He kicked. He kicked a lot. When you get shot, that stuff you see on Hoot Gibson doesn't work. When you're hit, you're hit. You kick. You feel that stuff burning through your flesh. I know how it feels. I've been hit three times.

That's what really got to me - he was so big. I didn't expect that.

They were hard core, too. The enemy would do anything to win. You had to respect that. They believed in a cause. They had the support of the people. That's the key that we Americans don't understand. We can't do anything in the military unless we have the support of the people.

From "Bloods" by Wallace Terry

An iced drink and trousers ripped across the crotch

I continue to make my way south and east following a small road designed for pedestrians and scooters alongside a wide canal, busy as a highway with junks large and small. I ride for 30ks, gently, I hope, through their lives, observing the intimate details of domesticity as I pass. A woman makes a bed just metres from where I ride; another sweeps the road outside her home with a palm-frond broom, claiming this as her own. I feel like I am trespassing in her front yard. The road itself becomes a narrow, elongated path to their front doors - except there are no front doors, their lives open to those of us who pass by.

Because most of this land is covered by water, sometimes I pass right through businesses constructed across the levee, the narrow roadway passing, of necessity, through the middle. So I ride slowly through mills and storehouses while business continues around me.

In the midday heat I pause to photograph a half-laden junk moored to the canal edge and the owner waves me over. I leave the bike and teeter across a long bamboo pole tied to other poles sunk into the mud two metres below and step over the gunnels and into his boat-home. In the heat he wears only shorts, his skin smooth and hairless. He wipes a flat surface clean and I sit. Next to me is the thick metal shaft of the steering gear, attached on one side to the wheel, the other making a right-angled bend in a geared junction box and attached to the massive rudder. The junk is made of thick teak planks, the hold in front of the cabin half loaded with sacks of rice.

These vessels are robustly constructed. All those I have been able to look at closely have been perfectly dry with no seepage at all into the hold, no bilges to catch the accumulated water that will inevitably leak into a ship.

The man and I look at one another and smile. We have no shared language so sign language will have to do.

Normally strangers in a situation like this will comment on the weather so I indicate by wiping my brow and fanning my face that it is hot. Immediately the man opens an insulated cooler box, lifts out a massive block of ice, hacks off a piece with a large knife, drops it into a bucket, pours water into it, swirls it about and then pours some into a plastic mug for me.

The sweat runs down his bare chest. He pours himself a mug of the cold water and we sit in silence a while. Then he takes out a needle and thread and shows me a pair of trousers ripped across the crotch and I laugh. He begins to sew...

A little later I stop to look at a small ship-repair yard. Two junks have been winched out of the water for repair and restoration. The thin aluminium sheets that clad the bottoms of most junks have been peeled away to reveal the raw wood beneath. Some rotten planks have been removed and replaced, the timber cut and shaped from thick, rough-cut planks of teak. A large, hand-cranked winch has been used to haul the boats out of the canal on metal rails; from one boat the engine has been removed, suspended from a crude hoist, lifted with the aid of block and tackle. The tools that I see lying about are basic and could have been found in any workshop during the last century, but the work is neat and precise.

A small man in his thirties notices me poking about and greets me. He too wears only shorts and sandals because of the heat. An older man with a wispy beard relaxes at a table in the sun, tea and glasses on a metal tray in front of him. The younger man invites me to join them and I sit.

Again, we have no shared language. I attempt "England", pointing to myself, and then try "Manchester" - words that usually evoke a response - but there is no recognition on either face. The old man pours tea and we sit quietly in the sun and drink a few glasses in companionable silence.

When the young man picks up his glass, I notice that two fingers of his right hand have been partially severed and have healed at right angles. In the workshop there is a large circular saw driven by an electric motor with wicked-looking teeth and I assume that to be the culprit. The misalignment of the fingers suggests that, after the accident, the fingers were left to heal on their own without recourse to professional help.

I know I have made this point before, perhaps a few times in my travels, but it bears repeating: How is it that the poorest in society are so often the most generous and hospitable? Perhaps what makes the difference is time. They often have lots of it whereas our pressurised lives leave little space for generosity towards others; our self-absorption will often exclude those whom we regard as peripheral to our objectives, our designs. And iced water or a glass of tea really costs nothing. But the principal is clear: we have lost something precious which these people still hold dear: the willingness to share the little they have with a passing stranger.

* * * * *

Now we had this dog to sniff out VC. Normally he would walk the point with the dog handler. His handler, Corporal Rome from Baltimore, swore Hobo could smell the Vietnamese a mile away. If he smelled one, his hair went straight. You know something was out there.

One time, when we were walking a trail near Con Thien, this guy was in this tree. At first we thought he was one of the local indigenous personnel, like the ARVN. He turned out to be something else. He had his pyjamas on and his army trousers. He wasn't firing. He was just sitting there. Hobo just ran up in that tree, reached back, and tore off his uniform. He was armed with an AK47. Hobo took that away from him, threw him up in the air, and grabbed him by the neck and started dragging him. We learned a lot from that guy. You put a dog on a guy, and he'll tell you anything you want to know.

We used to dress Hobo up with a straw hat on his head and shades on. All of us had shades. And we used to take pictures of Hobo. And sit him on the chopper. And he'd be in the back of the chopper with his shades on and his hat, and he would smile at us...

...(One day) Hobo signalled the ambush, but nobody paid any attention. We walked into the ambush. A machine gun hit them. Oliver got shot dead three times in the head, three times in the chest, and six times in the leg. Rome got hit in the leg. Hobo got shot in the side, but even though he was hit, he got on top of Rome. The only person that Hobo allowed to go over there and touch Rome was me.

From "Bloods" by Wallace Terry

Prelude to the inevitable

Reaching the built-up outer reaches of Ho Chi Minh City, I begin once again to battle my way through increasingly clogged traffic, made worse by the low-altitude heat and humidity. But finally I break free and find my way onto a newly built motorway. At last I begin to make good progress north until a man in a uniform flags me down, informing me that it is illegal for motorcycles to use this road. I have to get off.

Normally this would not be a problem; you just find a smaller road around. But in a land with seemingly more water than land, cut through with a myriad rivers and canals, it becomes more difficult. Every road I take seems to lead me to a bridgeless barrier of water. Eventually, though, I make it through and, climbing slowly, I leave the delta behind.

But the land is still heavily populated and I am forced to ride in a state of hyper-alertness. There can be no lack of vigilance. Scooters can - and do - suddenly appear from any direction, from either side of the road; slower scooters block the road in front, faster ones whip past from behind; trucks flash their lights, hoot and then fill the oncoming lane with their lethal bulk, forcing you to take evasive action onto the hard shoulder; bicycles and push-carts suddenly materialise out of the melee while other scooters, finding themselves on the wrong side of the road, ride straight at you using the hard shoulder. This is understandable, I suppose; safer than attempting to cross but still potentially lethal. Traffic roundabouts are a circus: very wide, no lanes, one can encounter traffic coming at you from anywhere. Approach and negotiate with caution. It's a death zone.

I become aware of my eyes darting about constantly, looking for anything that seems to be on a trajectory that will intersect mine or for a driver or rider suddenly about to do something stupid - the impact sound of the scooter crash a few days before, the bodies lying in the road, one not moving, an ever-present memory.

Realising the danger I am in, I consciously instruct my brain to focus. Some of you might remember that diagram in the old motorcycle training manual that shows a rider with multiple lines coming from his eyes instructing him to be aware, simultaneously, of, here, a child playing with a ball next to the road; there, a pedestrian about to cross; ahead, a car indicating right; another person about to open a car door and so on, suggesting that a responsible rider ought to be aware of all of these things all the time if he wants to stay alive. Here, in Vietnam, it is the same except multiplied manifold times: youth on a scooter riding at silly speed weaving through traffic... old woman wobbling on a bicycle... massive truck flashing its lights, already turning into oncoming traffic, shouldering scooters aside in the bow wave of its horn... man on a scooter with young man riding pillion holding two large panes of glass sideways in his bare hands... old man pushing heavily-laden three-wheeler in the middle of the traffic... 4X4 coming up fast behind, hooting and flashing lights (tempted to give him the finger but feel it's wiser to keep both hands on the bars)... scooter coming straight at me on the wrong side of the road - which way is he going to pass?... woman pulls out to overtake extended family on a scooter, rider holding sleeping child in the crook of one arm; pull out to miss her - just enough space between me and an oncoming bus... bus driver wafts his hand out the window - he's pulling across to drop off a passenger... scooter doing a U-turn right in front of me... another scooter heading at me at an angle from the other side of the road - if I keep going, he'll just pass behind me... old woman steps out into the traffic with determined gait - I'm going to cross now, traffic or not, her body language informs us and the scooters and trucks and cars flow around her... scooter stopped half way across the road, an abortive attempt to u-turn, now waiting for a break in the traffic that builds up around her like a wave...

And so it goes on, mile after mile of milling vehicles, every moment a potential collision averted.

Finally the traffic thins. I cross a wide estuary where families live in floating houses, moored in ordered gatherings like satellite villages in the water, each house buoyed on a frame kept afloat by empty oil drums. Outside, grids of nets, about 8m X 8m, hold fish whose scales flash pink in the sun. Crude water craft - a metal platform holding together 44-gal drums and driven by a motor - ply the waters carrying produce.

I ride on, the road beginning to climb. The water disappears and tall trees bring welcome shade.

The air begins to cool...

* * * * *

Sampan Valley was serious. It was supposed to have been a simple mission. It turned out to be a major operation, 'cos they knew we were comin'. I mean, they're not crazy. I mean they weren't a bunch of yahoos out there trying to wage war. They knew we lift at eleven, because they can see us in the mess hall. They smell us taking a shower. They can smell our soap. They smell our cologne. They smell us gettin' dressed. And we get prepped up like we gettin' ready to go to a serious party. You comb your hair. I mean you're at war combing our hair.

We lost a lot of good people that night. Good people. Because the hierarchy decided that this is what we going to do. And the

Viet Cong know it.

We lost four ships that night, and heavy damage to Puff the Magic Dragon. And when you lose two Cobras, the Colonel has to explain, 'cos you don't lose Cobras. And they lost two that night. Two.

From "Bloods" by Wallace Terry

Just wearing a red sock

I write this lying in a hospital bed in Da Lac.

A man with a gentle face looks after me with the concern and attention a mother would give to her sick child. His son, early twenties, lies in the bed next to mine. Often he, the father, comes over to me, sits on the side of my bed and rests his hand on my knee, looking into my face with eyes so gentle I feel embarrassed. Last night he fed me - no food is supplied in Vietnamese hospitals; relatives and friends need to bring food in. I don't know what happens to people like me who are alone.

In the bed opposite, a young woman sits with her daughter, about five years old, cares for her, sleeps with her. The child's head is shaved bare; a recently sutured wound makes raw knots from her neck to the top of her head. A sweet child, she doesn't cry or complain.

In the far corner a very thin man looks after his young wife who has been involved in a motorcycle accident. She doesn't look well; she has scabbed grazes on her face, up one arm and down her legs. She sleeps most of the time, her husband sitting silent next to her on the bed, wiping her face with a cloth.

The last bed is taken by a young woman who was brought in with two friends late last night. Another motorcycle accident. She was hit by a car and is covered with raw abrasions. Her two friends slept the night on her bed, one next to her, the other curled up between their feet. This, too, seems to be common practice in Vietnamese hospitals. Since being admitted I have seen no nurses. Friends, husbands, parents look after, feed, wash and sleep in the same beds as those for whom they care. It's a happy, bustling atmosphere, everyone mucking in, washing, preparing food, chatting. A different way of doing things.

To go back, then...It was inevitable, I suppose. Riding along a busy street, minding my own business, a young woman on a scooter suddenly came at me at an angle from the side, the trajectory of which meant that a collision was certain. I tried to turn with her but it was too late. We hit hard; she went down. I took the impact on my foot and right forearm. The collision knocked me across the road into the path of oncoming traffic but, fortunately, at that moment, the road was clear. No massive truck flashing its lights and bulldozing its way through. I would have been dead, then.

I hadn't gone down but I knew it was going to be bad. I was vaguely aware of the young woman trying to pick her bike up off the road, bits of broken plastic scattered about.

I sat for a few moments on my bike, in the road, not wanting to look, knowing it wasn't going to be pretty.

Eventually I looked down. Blood was seeping out of a ragged hole in the side of my boot.

I got off the bike and sat down on the pavement. A few people paused to watch. Then I loosened the laces and pulled off the boot and then the blood-soaked sock. There was a deep gash in the side of my foot and a horrible looking dent in the flesh. Blood dripped into the dust.

Just then my Good Samaritan arrived. An American woman of Indian decent - not Native American, from India - crouched at my side and said, "Don't worry, I'm going to look after you. Don't worry about anything..."

She and her driver helped me to their 4X4, left idling in the road. Inside it was air-conditioned. Her driver was speaking to people outside on the pavement. Then he got back into the car, said something to the woman and we drove off.

"There's a clinic a few miles away," she told me. "Don't worry, everything's going to be all right."

On the way, which was further than her driver implied, she told me about how she had seen me sitting on the roadside. "Stop, he's bleeding!" she had said to her driver.

"No," he replied, "he's just wearing a red sock."

"No," she insisted. "He's bleeding. Stop!"

He did. While the woman was getting me into her hired car, the driver had negotiated with a shopkeeper to look after my bike and luggage and the lady would pay when he came later to fetch the bike.

We arrived at the clinic. The woman helped me in. It was clean and looked professional. The driver asked me for my bike keys and disappeared. A nurse arrived and, later, a doctor. They seemed concerned and treated me kindly, personally. X-Rays were taken and revealed what I expected: a shattered patella.

A short while later the driver returned with my keys and told me that my bike was parked outside. I thanked him and the woman, who offered to pay the hospital charge. I assured her I had money and, reluctantly, after fussing about me a while longer, they left.

A pretty nurse bandaged my foot and the doctor informed me that he couldn't treat me any further; I need to go to a big hospital, he informed me - the closest one is in Da Lat, 150ks away.

I paid for the treatment - X-Rays and treating the wound - just under £2.00, gingerly hobbled out the front door of the clinic and climbed back on the bike. Then, tentatively, keeping well clear of cars, trucks, bicycles, pedestrians, scooters and sharp right turns that might scrape my bandaged foot along the road, I make my slow way towards Da Lat and a hospital.

It is a pleasant ride through the low highlands and there is little pain. A few hours later, when close to Da Lat, I interrogate my GPS and it informs me that there are four hospitals in the city. I navigate my way through heavy traffic to two of them before I am given directions to the correct one.

Again I am absorbed into its warm embrace and looked after like a wayward, injured child. A nurse gives me pyjamas; my belongings are itemised and sealed into a bag.

The surgeon who treats me speaks some English and he takes me carefully through what he does. First a local anaesthetic into my foot and a nurse swabs out the wound. He takes forceps and lifts the flaps of skin. My tendon has been severed, he tells me. I am able to sit up and watch. He shows me the cut tendon, gripped in a pair of forceps; it is thicker than I had imagined, pale, yellow-white like a fat earthworm. Deftly he sews it together again then asks me to wiggle my toes. I do and my little toe moves. He smiles, pleased with his work. The toe is somewhat shorter than it had been the day before.

He sews up the gashes and wraps my foot in a half cast. I am wheeled through bare corridors to the great interest of those hanging about waiting for their loved ones to heal.

Then into the ward and an empty bed. The young woman in the bed opposite points me out to her shaven-headed daughter and the little girl laughs. The father of the young lad greets me. He tells me his name is Due Hien. He is fifty years old. His cheek is swollen and his ear covered with plaster. Motorbike accident, he tells me using sign language. His son, 24, is called Viet Hung.

And I am absorbed into this microcosm and made to feel at home. A passing woman brings me water in a plastic cup and waits while I drink; a man offers me a small carton of milk. I haven't eaten in 24 hours and am hungry. No one brings me food. Late in the evening, Due Hien gives me some Vietnamese take-away in a paper bag that someone has not eaten. I accept it gladly. They all watch as I eat, pleased for me.

But Due doesn't just give the food to me - he serves me, sitting on the side of my bed, opening this and that, pouring the small plastic bag of soup into a bowl, fetching me a spoon, encouraging me to eat with gestures and smiles.

He has no English at all; in fact, none in the ward knows a single word. So all our communication is in sign language and we get by. There is not much of the basics that can't be conveyed with gestures and facial expressions.

When he returns to his son's bed I look at him, this gentle-faced man who takes such care of me. And I reflect on the tragic irony: This man was the enemy - not to me growing up in South Africa but, to most of those living in the West, Due was the epitome of all that was hated and feared - the ugly face of Communism, the villain who turned his inscrutable face away when you entered his village and then shot you in the back before disappearing into the bush or deep underground, the angular-faced caricature, without feeling, emotion or any attempt at three-dimensionality, mown down indiscriminately by gun-toting marines in a hundred gung-ho, kill-all-the-baddies films.

I continue to watch him and when his kindly face is averted and at rest, when he is not looking at me, I see something in the angular planes of his face that reveals the strength and resilience of his race.

Later, an official looking man enters the ward and stands at the foot of my bed. Unlike most Vietnamese men, he is large, well fed and wears a suit. He greets me by name and asks if I'm all right.

I assure him I am and wonder who he is and what he wants.

"I am from the Ministry of the Interior," he informs me and I am suddenly afraid that he has come to arrest me - leaving the scene of an accident, insurance...

"Do you have an International Drivers' Licence?" he asks and I tell him, No, only my UK licence. He nods, his face impassive.

But then he smiles and tells me that he has just come to make sure I have everything I need and that all is well. I assure him that I have been treated with kindness. He shakes my hand and leaves. I am relieved.

Much later, everyone settles down for the night, the ill as well as their friends and family, curling themselves in tangled piles on and into the beds.

I sleep well.

In the morning, Due brings me tea and offers to go out onto the street and get me something to eat. He suggests rice but I ask him for fruit and coffee. I give him money and in a short time he is back. Again, he doesn't just hand me the food, he feeds me as a parent would an ailing child. He peels my apple with a penknife, cores it and cuts it into segments which he presents to me, one piece at a time, like an offering. I accept, embarrassed by this expression of care from a total stranger.

Later a stern-looking matron stands at the door and issues orders: Due must get off my bed and sit on a plastic stool; the young mother must get off her daughter's bed while she is eating. We all snap to attention. This matron is a woman you don't want to mess with. And she doesn't smile.

That's how matrons in hospitals ought to be; make even junior doctors tremble.

At mid-morning my surgeon enters and greets me with a hearty, "Good morning, Lawrence!" and watches while a junior nurse removes my half cast and then stands back. All the inhabitants of the ward get off their beds and gather round to watch. It's like a floor show; theatre in the round.

My surgeon asks them to stand back and he checks my wound. All seems well.

"Some skin will die," he tells me, "but that is normal."

He informs me I will have to stay in hospital at least five days but I shake my head. I need to continue my travels, I tell him - today. We discuss this for a while, he explaining that it would be far better for me to end my trip immediately and fly home. I am adamant that I will complete it.

Reluctantly he nods and tells me that he will make sure I have the necessary medicine.

As soon as the surgeon leaves, Due and his son invite me to come with them. I follow them down a corridor to a large room, bare except for some plastic chairs and tables. Outside the door is a sign that says "KAN TIN" - a typically Vietnamese monosyllabic transliteration.

We order coffee and drink it together, slowly.

Back in the ward, I find that the woman and the little girl are now in my bed. They shift up for me and I sit. A middle-aged man has been brought in with a broken collarbone. There's no bed blocking in Vietnam; you just shift up and share, men, women, children. And why not? It works. Goodness, imagine the outrage in the UK!

I point to the man's shoulder. "Motorcycle?" I ask, making the universally accepted two-handed throttle-grip sign.

His wife, who is with him, nods, grim-faced. He is in a lot of pain.

Later, my surgeon tells me that the previous week he treated a Spanish biker with a badly broken leg. It seems that Vietnam's reputation as one of the most dangerous places to ride a bike is well founded.

The accident: I can't say I'm glad it happened; I'd much rather it hadn't. But sitting here sharing my hospital bed with a stoical little girl with a recently-sutured scar from her neck to the top of her head wearing bright yellow Minnie Mouse tights and a yellow "Hello Kitty" vest who sits next to me playing with her Minions hand-cranked plastic fan has given me a deeper insight into the lives of these good people, built up in my mind more layers in the patina of my experience - and this, I believe, is what makes travel in a foreign land so special: getting away from the places frequented by tourists, by our own kind, those who speak our language and share our life philosophies, to where the ordinary folk of another land live and interact and involve themselves in the mundane, day-to-day process of living.

And lonely and difficult as it can be sometimes, travelling alone has its own special qualities: had I been with a group of friends, they would have taken care of me, not the local people, the Indian/American woman and her driver, Hue and his son... And I would have been denied that special privilege of being taken under the wings of local folk.

But I am determined to leave so, when the morning begins to pass, I get dressed, pack away my things and ask the matron whether I can go. She takes me to an office and I sign some papers. She asks me to pay and I take out my wallet. I don't know what to expect. There have been stories, travellers' tales about doctors retaining passports until exorbitant fees have been paid.

An itemised bill is printed: two million Dong. I do a quick mental calculation - about $100. I pay with a light heart, leave money with Due so he can buy coffee for the patients in my ward, and say my farewells. As I limp down the corridor towards the exit, my surgeon calls out to me. He gives me a script and shakes me by the hand, wishing me well. I must visit a chemist, he tells me, and buy the medicine, take the antibiotics and keep the wound clean.

Outside the front door of the hospital is my bike. All my kit is still there, safe and untouched.

Gingerly I swing my bandaged foot over the seat, toe the road lightly and start the bike.

Once again I am free...

* * * * *

Well, the Viet Cong came in. They came in through the main gate of the base dressed as ARVNs. A couple of truckloads. They put a Quad 50 on top of that big water tower. It meant they could shoot straight down the flight line. So you can't get a chopper or anything off the ground.

And they were coming across the barbed wire with AK47s, with old French rifles, crudely made grenades, pitchforks - anything they could use to kill, maim, or wound.

Anything had a slant in their eyes out on the barbed wire that night was in trouble. They were the enemy. They was supposed to be dead.

They left about 400 people on the barbed wire that night. When we pulled the bodies out, there was three people that worked in the kitchen in battalion headquarters. They served the food to the officers. One of the cooks from our mess hall was there. Some of the people that owned the little shops that was just outside the base. Some of the boom-de-boom girls. Some of the owners of the boom-de-boom clubs. Some of the guys that you see in the clubs that just seem to come in and just be sitting there. And the people that worked in the barber shop. Two of them. And the girls who polished our shoes and washed our clothes.

From "Bloods" by Wallace Terry

Complicit in the murder of children

The road from Da Lat to the coast at Phan Rang over the Ngoan Muc Pass ought to be registered on The Hundred Best Motorcycle Roads, if there is such a list. It's about 100ks of pure enjoyment, the kind of road where you think: If I had the time, I'd just turn round at the bottom and ride back up - and then down again, of course - just because I can.

Obviously, being a mountain pass, it winds. I wouldn't suggest its inclusion in The Best Hundred if it didn't. But what makes it so special are a number of things that, cumulatively, make the road such a joy: the surface is good with only a few pot-holes; being up at 1900m and slowly descending, the temperature is cool; there is very little traffic and almost no trucks or buses; until you reach the lower sections of the pass near the coast, there are no towns or villages - not even Montagnard settlements; there are no police (well, none that I saw) and, finally, the road makes its way through natural forest, untouched and inviolate except, in the lower reaches, where the destructive and pestilential practice of slash and burn has begun and the clear sky is blurred with smoke from the fires. Riding through the upper reaches, the canopy unbreached and dark green, tall hardwoods breaking through every now and then, you realise just how much of this forest has already been lost. Once, most of the country was covered just like this; now, except for small pockets, it's gone.

My smashed foot is vulnerable. It is protected - if one can call it that - by a thin, L-shaped cast just millimetres thick, held in place with a bandage. My toes stick out. I ride carefully; the thought of a fall onto a bare foot with shattered bones and wounds newly sutured makes me shudder. I favour my front brake. I can use the broken foot to depress the foot brake but my control is uncertain. When leaning into right-handers I sometimes lift my foot off the peg so my bare toes don't scrape the tar.

As I descend, the temperature soars again and I feel my skin start to burn. A terrible heat, even with the moving air from the bike. But once I reach the coast, the cooling influence of the sea moderates the temperature and I ride along Highway 1 through beautiful scenery: mountains on my left disappearing into the blue of distance, hazed with cloud and smoke; the white, palm-fringed beaches on my right, small sheltered bays protecting moored boats, red-and-blue painted as all water craft are here, bobbing in the wind, their graceful lines and painted eyes making them things of beauty. On either side of the road, fields of newly harvested wheat lie waterlogged, the domain of thousands of excited, dabbling ducks.

Then past Cam Ranh Bay. I don't stop. A naturally protected harbour - in fact, one of the best natural harbours in the whole of South Asia - Cam Ranh Bay has been used as a deep-water anchorage by Vietnamese, Russian, Japanese and American warships as the tide of influence in this area ebbed and flowed. The bay was developed by the Americans into their largest Marine base during the war and they held it from 1964 until their ignominious leaving in 1973. Here they also built a major airport and, for many newly drafted troops, the bay and the mountains and forests inland were their first experience of Vietnam. Many commented on the heat and the humidity that hit them like a punch in the face as they stepped off the plane. Referred to as Vietnam's Hawaii, the sheltered beaches in the bay were ideal for troops relaxing during periods of R&R.

I stop at a chemist to buy the medication prescribed for my wound and press on until after four, finding a pleasant motel just off the road.

Off the bike, I find walking difficult and painful.

Later, having showered and dressed my wound, I eat roasted corn on the cob with a family who speak no English, the full moon bright in the warm sky.

And then the peace is shattered by the brain-numbing beat of a karaoke bar...

In retrospect, my time at the karaoke bar gave me another great insight into the art of communicating without spoken language. Picture the scene: I sit at a small table in an open-sided veranda, roofed with corrugated iron, assuming it to be a restaurant (it isn't, but I only find that out later). On a small stage, two young men set up their instruments, an electric guitar and keyboard. At another table, a middle-aged woman and whom I assume to be her two teenage children. They stare at me and smile a lot. I smile back.

When no one comes to serve me, I mime my desire for food.

They giggle and discuss me but remain seated.

I persist, miming desperate hunger.

They point at a sign on the wall telling me, I think, that it closes at seven. I am relieved, as it's just turned 6.30: just in time to order my supper. I nod my understanding and again indicate my desire to be fed. (I assume, in retrospect, that they were telling me that the mayhem that in Vietnam goes under the term "karaoke" began at 7.)

"Feed me," I mime again, feeling like Audrey in The Little Shop of Horrors.

Realising that I am serious, they inform me (in Vietnamese) what food is available.

I look blank.

Perplexed, they summon youngest son, the intellectual one. He gets a piece of paper (with complicated Maths sums on the reverse side) and writes something in Vietnamese. Why he feels that writing it down will enable me to understand it better than when spoken I do not know.

"Brilliant!" I exclaim, using the time-honoured double thumbs-up and knowing that this is as close as I will get to knowing what I am ordering. "Perfect, just what I wanted. I'll have that."

The older woman raises two fingers - D20,000.

I nod. Great price for whatever it is I have just ordered.

Mum, who controls the money, extricates a purse from her bosom and hands some notes to older son who gets on his scooter and disappears. He's going to the village, I assume.

It is only at this moment that I begin to suspect that this is not a restaurant. Oops.

I sit and listen to the two young men tuning their instruments. They have been doing this for twenty minutes now, independently of each other, at full volume. The woman and her daughter watch me.

After ten minutes older son returns, looking sad. He reports back to mum who tells me that whatever younger son wrote on his piece of paper is no longer on the menu.

I look sad.

They confer.

Younger son brings his piece of paper again, writes more Vietnamese words and, with a flourish, shows them to me.

"Yes," I agree, looking at the meaningless writing full of little accents and things, "that would be great. Perfect! Just what I would have chosen myself." Another double-handed thumbs-up.

The older woman, with a deprecatory smile, holds up four fingers. D40,000. I do a quick calculation: $2. Yes, I think I can manage that. I nod and give her the thumbs up.

Once again, money is transferred from bosom to older son. He roars off on his scooter. Ten minutes later (the two lads still tuning up) he returns carrying a plastic bag. Inside, two smaller plastic bags, one containing hot soup, the other noodles. A bowl is produced. I tip in my noodles and then pour the soup on top, burning my fingers. Watching me, they offer a commiseratory smile.

Then I notice that the soup is full of little creatures with their hands upraised, as if they are crying, "Please, don't hurt us."

I cannot eat them. They are baby squid. I feel as if I am complicit in the murder of children...

* * * * *

And we got hit. And it was like here we go trees. The blade went. You know, the main rotary. But the pilot knew what to do, and we broke through the trees constantly, constantly. I was in the front seat, and you constantly had trees coming. You sitting there in that little plastic bubble. Something that's 37 inches wide. You sitting in the nose. It's like I wonder if Hughes did this right. If this s'posed to be a single piece. Is there a seam in the middle. Am I going to be going off one way or the other? And the tail hit, and we slid down the side of the tree.

I asked the plot, "Can you move?"

"No."

I can't get out, so I had to break the canopy because the lock doesn't work. I got out the side, and laid down. And I thought, Well, goddam. Let me regroup.

I'm bleeding. Not only am I bleedin', excrement is coming out of the wound, which means that my lower intestines are damaged. It's oozing out. It don't run out. All these little enzymes are just rolling down over your clothes.

I was first concerned that I was gon' to bleed to death. My pulse was up, and my body hadn't responded to shock yet. But the main artery wasn't severed. A round took out the left side of my prostate gland, came through my lower intestines, and came out the left hip.

The pilot was bleedin' from the mouth. That meant blood had gotten into his stomach. I thought his ribs had punctured somethin', but he was still breathin'.

I cut him out, got him out the back seat. And dragged him away, 'cause, you know, the fuel can blow anytime.

He can't move his arms. When the turbine had exploded, his seat - the back seat - jerked and his back was gone.

I covered him up to stop the shock and gave him some morphine. I jacked him right up to the ceiling. We ain't had no water.

Then I dropped a grenade in the cockpit to destroy the maps. The fuel blew, and that will take care of the mini-guns and the rest of it.

The first thing you do on your way down is turn a little device on that's like a homing device. So somebody knew we were down, but nobody knew where. Of course, the hostile force knew, and you could sense they were out there.

We talked and talked. I had to keep him awake, because he was keeping me awake. And amazingly enough, we talked about screwing. 'Bout all the fine dames we ever knew. We lied about everybody we wished we could have had. We weren't bragging, we were lying. And he talked about what life was like when he was a kid. What it was like for me. And what we doin' out here.

It was 13 hours when they spotted us. They spotted us through an opening in the trees that we made when we fell. A couple of Phantoms came and laid down the firepower to get rid of everybody that was within distance of bein' able to pluck you off. And then the Cobras did their thing. Then they brought in that Chinook, and dropped the basket. And there come Rosey down the ropes. "Goddam, boy," he says. "Good to see your ass."

The medic came down and said, "I think the war is over for you."

From "Bloods" by Wallace Terry

A lifestyle choice

The air cools as I continue travelling north along the coast road. I overtake large-wheeled, wooden carts drawn by plodding water buffalo, slow and ponderous, as if from some forgotten age. Mango trees with their dark-green, waxy leaves line the road while off shore, fishing boats are moored, their huge square nets suspended over the water on poles. On the verge, hay from newly harvested rice has been spread out to dry. The roadside, despite the bellowing traffic just a few feet away, has become a convenient winnowing surface. Various grains, once removed from their husks, are laid out in the road on cloths to dry then swept into neat piles with grass brooms and scooped into plastic buckets. The leftover hay is loaded onto the backs of small 50cc three-wheelers, the loads impossibly high, hooding the riders like thick grass cowls.

There is something essentially beautiful about fishing boats moored on a calm sea, palm trees, off-shore islands, bush-covered mountains dropping steeply into the water.

So, despite my injured foot, I can't restrain myself from following a narrow footpath down to the beach where at least a hundred fishing boats and small, round coracles are moored, some pulled up onto the sand for careening or repair. I hobble up to the boats and watch as the fishermen work: an old man crouches inside the hull of his boat, working on the engine. Inside it is cramped and dark. I notice that the drive shaft has been clamped together with two pieces of wood, bolted and wired. While I watch, he adds more wire to the joint and tightens it with a pair of pliers. A young boy paints a mast red; a group of men strip barnacles from the bottom of a newly beached boat with metal scrapers, filling the air with the rank smell of underwater things. Heavy-weave fibreglass cloth is being laid over the outer planks of another boat and painted with resin, its distinctive smell strong in the air - a modern solution, I suppose, to leaking seams and rotting planks. In one boat, planks have been replaced, the new ones pale and rough still, slotted into place like jigsaw pieces. All the larger boats have banks of lights attached to the rigging for night fishing.

Back on the road, I notice a fat woman riding a small scooter, her flesh red and puffy from the sun. I am taken aback because the sight of anyone overweight in Vietnam is a rarity. Then I realise she is Western and I am ashamed.

After travelling through many countries inhabited by thin people, one comes to realise that, with a few exceptions, obesity is a lifestyle choice, an indulgence.

Eat less, exercise more. Sorted. It's not rocket science.

Sorry, touched a nerve...

* * * * *

One time we were chasing a VC, and the VC run into this hole. The lieutenant wanted one of our men to crawl into the hole after him. In fact, he was telling this little brother, Bobby Williams from Philadelphia, because Bobby was the smallest one.

That was ridiculous. Because those tunnels may look like to be a little hole but may end up to be a total complex. Many times the holes are dug in off the entrance. VC go in and crawl into this little slot. If a man crawled in behind them, he were subject to get his head blown off.

I said, "Bobby, don't go in there. You crazy?"

So I said let's throw some fire in the hole as opposed to sending one of our men in that hole. Do that, and we'll pull Bobby out by his ankles and he won't have a head.

Bobby did not go in. And we put fire in the hole. And the VC did not come out.

From "Bloods" by Wallace Terry

My Lai and the sins of the world

Son My is probably better known to us in the West as My Lai. The very name ought to send shivers of shame through the soul of every American (and, through association, ours too).

I visit because I have to. It is a time of reflection as well as an apology for my belonging to the human race.

This place is the Auschwitz-Birkenau of Vietnam and its memory is just as carefully preserved. We ought to approach here on our hands and knees...

This is not a book about My Lai and most of you will be well aware of what happened here. It led to the revealing to a shocked world the atrocities of American soldiers against Vietnamese civilians, atrocities that, as the war continued year after bloody year without an end in sight, were becoming the norm rather than the exception.

My Lai revealed to the Americans that they were no longer the good guys fighting against a wicked enemy; never again could they claim to be the military embodiment of the white-suited cowboy with his six-gun always ready to stand up for the poor and down-trodden; that he was, in fact, as weak and fallible and corrupt and murderously violent as the bad guys from whom we always expected him to defend us.

My Lai taught Americans that it was no longer acceptable to use their power and technological advantage to interfere in the lives of people they didn't understand; that good intentions don't always result in gratitude.

Hidden from the American public, these atrocities against the Vietnamese people had been going on for a long time, tacitly approved - if not encouraged - by those in authority, who just wanted this unwelcome war to end; leaders who had become increasingly disillusioned as they realised that the people they were supposedly defending seemed, perversely, to be working against them.

Very briefly, this is what happened:

On the morning of March 16, 1968, helicopters landed soldiers from Charlie Company of the 1st Brigade of the 23rd Americal Infantry Division near the hamlet of Son My in the Quang Ngai Province of Central Vietnam, close to the village of My Lai.

Charlie Company had recently suffered a number of casualties, including five dead, and the soldiers were angry and out for revenge. The recent Tet Offensive had clearly demonstrated that the North Vietnamese were nowhere near defeat and the enemy's unconventional tactics, the deadly booby traps and land mines that were killing and maiming their mates were sapping morale. They needed to strike back at an unseen enemy who seemed to be able to kill their soldiers at will and then disappear. Brutal reprisals against any civilians who were suspected of helping the VC had become routine and seemingly tolerated by those in command. The opinion amongst many of the soldiers was that they could act with impunity; what happens in the field, stays in the field became their mantra.

On the eve of the mission, Capt. Ernest Medina told his troops that all of the villagers would have left for the market by the time they attacked so that anyone they found still in the village would be VC sympathisers and could be legitimately killed. But, according to those who testified later, Capt. Medina went further, ordering his troops to destroy "everything in the village that was walking, crawling or growing"; this included all animals and crops, the burning of houses and polluting the wells. Furthermore, Brigade Commander Colonel Oran K. Henderson met with the men before they set off, instructing them to "Go in there aggressively, close with the enemy and wipe them out for good."

These angry and bitter young men, whose average age was just 19, had clearly been primed for murder and implicitly knew that they had been given carte blanche to do whatever they wanted.

And they did.

By 7.30 on Saturday morning, the 100 troops from Charlie Company had landed and were in place. Some women were seen working in the rice paddies and they were fired upon; a number of villagers were rounded up. According to witnesses, a soldier stabbed one of them with a bayonet then pushed a man down a well and threw a hand grenade in after him.

Suddenly the soldiers went berserk, killing unarmed men and women, children and babies. Women and girls were raped, houses set alight and those who attempted to escape were gunned down. Women who covered their babies with their bodies were shot and the babies killed if still alive.

A group of sixty villagers, men, women and children, had been rounded up. Lt William Calley approached them and ordered his men to kill them. When one soldier refused, Calley started shooting himself. Similar atrocities were taking place throughout the village: men, women and children beaten, clubbed and bayoneted to death. Some of the bodies were later found to have been mutilated.

While the villagers were being murdered, WO1 Hugh Thompson, a helicopter pilot, was flying in close support of the attacking troops. Seeing what was happening, he radioed for help then landed alongside a ditch full of dead and wounded. He called to some soldiers standing around to help him get the wounded into his helicopter but one, a sergeant, told him he would "help them out of their misery" then began shooting into the ditch.

WO1 Thompson took off and saw a group of villagers hiding in a bunker, surrounded by US troops. He landed close to them, got out of his helicopter and ordered the soldiers not to fire. His crew, who had also exited the aircraft, drew their weapons. Thompson told the attacking troops that if anyone attempted to harm the villagers, he and his crew would shoot them. He then asked the soldiers to help him and his crew but was told that the only way to get the Vietnamese out was "with a grenade". While his crew kept their guns on the other US soldiers, Thompson managed to persuade those who were hiding in the bunker to come out, then he stood guard over them while they were flown to safety. It took two trips to get them away.

For their actions on that day, Thompson and his crew were ostracised by other soldiers and even denounced as traitors by several US Congressmen. It took thirty years before their bravery was honoured; they were decorated for "shielding non-combatants from harm in a war zone".

There is some debate about just how many villagers were killed in Son My. The Vietnamese, however, have no doubts. On a plaque in the museum, five hundred and four names are recorded; details include the place and manner of death of each villager.

For many years the massacre was hushed up despite a number of witnesses informing their senior officers and writing to congressmen, revealing that massacres just like this one were taking place all the time.

Eventually, as it always does, the truth came out. Americans had to admit, for the first time in their history, that they were no longer the innocent peacemakers of the world; their loss of virginity was humiliating and many tried to deny it, but the terrible truth was laid bare during the trials for the whole world to see.

Twenty-six officers were charged but only Lt William Calley, who seemed to have been selected as a scapegoat, was convicted. The charge: the murder of twenty-two unarmed civilians. He was sentenced to life imprisonment but this was later reduced to house arrest. After only three and a half years, President Nixon gave Calley a presidential pardon and he was free.

The village has become a mausoleum. I walk through the entrance and past the museum. To the left, on a well-tended lawn, two mass graves have been marked. Scattered throughout the area are low, crumbling walls. Their square shape reminds me of the outline of simple huts - and this is what they turn out to be, each with a plaque outside detailing who lived there at the time of the massacre and how they died. Parents, grandparents, little children, each given the dignity of a name.

A cement path leads the visitor between the remains of the huts. There are strange markings on its surface. I pause and look closely: in the wet concrete the bare footprints of villagers can be seen, adult and child. Over them, in places obliterating them, are the large, deep imprints of boots - the boots of American soldiers who walked here in the early morning of Saturday, March 16, 1968, bitter and frustrated at the near impossibility of fighting an enemy that they couldn't see, an enemy who hid in plain sight, who didn't wear uniforms, who smiled and waved and laid booby traps and mines that blew the legs off their friends and dug holes filled with pointed punji sticks; soldiers who had tacitly been given permission to kill anything that moved by their officers; angry young men who were looking for someone to blame.

Outside some huts, original trees that survived the burning are given their own plaques. The ditch where the bodies were piled is still there. Further back a memorial wall drips a mosaic of blood while above, a single American warplane with open mouth and long yellow teeth in the shape of fingers and bullets, bristling with bombs and rockets, dives onto a huddled group of women and children. Alongside it, a statue showing villagers comforting the dying while a woman, cradling a dead child, raises a clenched fist in defiance. At the foot of the statue, fresh flowers lie amongst the burnt-out ends of incense sticks.

I leave the grounds and enter the museum. It spares no punches. Like the displays of shoes and empty suitcases and glasses and hair and artificial limbs at Auschwitz-Birkenau in Poland, here are put on display the toys, dolls, marbles, plates and other personal possessions collected after the massacre, each labelled with the name of the owner and how he or she was murdered. The captions to graphic photographs of dead and maimed bodies are blunt and, I believe, deserve to be quoted:

"US soldiers shooting farmers on the way to the rice fields"

"Various weapons used for killing 504 innocent people"

"Bullets of the gun AR15 used to shoot into civilians"

"The US soldiers' daggers used to stab into the abdomens of women and children"

"The US troop's mask used to avoid the poison when the soldier dropped the poison into villager's shelter"

"US soldiers reaching up every house of the villagers to murder them"

"US soldiers burning huts"

"US soldiers looking for air raid shelters of villagers to murder them"

"US soldiers piling thatches on bodies, burning all into ashes to destroy their traces of crime"

"The last moment of life of women and children under a silk-cotton tree before being murdered"

"Photo of two little boys. The older boy was covering up his younger brother. Then, they were finished off by American soldiers"

"The propeller of the 300kg bomb which US soldiers dropped down Son My village to destroy their crimes after massacre"

"The US army using tanks to plough the village to rub out their crime traces".

It is all carefully documented. There is no room for doubt. No Holocaust deniers here. It happened. Here is the bleak testimony of man's inhumanity to man; to the abhorrence of war; to the depravity of man.

A close-up photograph of Mrs Pham Thi Phan. She is a woman in her mid-fifties, hair long and greying. On her face a look of pained resignation. Not fear. There is in this face a dignity bred from generations of resisting oppression. Pressed into her temple, so hard that the skin of her cheek is puckered, is the barrel of a M16 rifle. Although the caption doesn't say it, she was killed. I found her name later on the list of the victims.

An old man, cradling one grandchild on his lap while another child holds onto his shoulder, their lives saved by two Vietnamese interpreters. Behind them, US soldiers range about, rifles in their hands.

Another photograph shows Herbert Carter, foot bandaged, being helped to a medivac helicopter by two other GIs. Official US accounts tell of a weapon "accidentally discharged while cleaning". Some of his fellow marines report that he deliberately shot himself in the foot because he could no longer bear to witness the murder going on around him. The caption to the photograph reads, in typical early Communist hyperbole: "Herbert Carter, a US soldier injuring himself in the foot for being terrified at the holocaust by his criminal partners."

On display, too, are more modern photographs in colour, showing old men, ex-US servicemen, some with missing limbs, laying wreaths at the memorial, their faces solemn and reflective.

Enough.

Absorbed and deeply reflective, I am no longer aware of the passing of time. Something makes me glance up from a photograph I do not want to look at but feel compelled to as an act of respect and I become aware of an old man, small and gently deferential, at my side. He points at his watch: it's five minutes to closing time.

I look about me one last time, reluctant to leave. Outside the sun is low on the horizon; the voices of children playing come clear in the still air.

The old man waits for me at the gate. I want to say something to him - but what?

Sorry?

Please accept my apology for the sins of the world?

As I ride out our eyes meet and briefly hold.

I am sure that he understands my need to be there.

* * * * *

One day in June my team went on a POW snatch. It was hot as hell. It felt like 120 degrees. I was wearing combat boots this time 'cause we could jump out a helicopter from 10 feet into the elephant grass. I landed on a punji stick. It was about two feet long, sticking up in the ground. I don't know if my weight or whatever pulled the stake loose. But I just kept running because there was no use stopping.

It went right through my boot, my foot, everything. It just protruded through the top of my boot. I couldn't get the boot off. And I was told not to pull it through the leather. The base said if it doesn't give you that much problem, don't mess with it. They would get me out as soon as possible, but not immediately, 'cause they couldn't jeopardise the mission by comin' back out and get us.

They didn't get me out for three days. My foot swell up inside my boot. They had to cut my boot off. It just happened that I was lucky that it wasn't human urine on the stake, or my foot would've been amputated from infection.

From "Bloods" by Wallace Terry

Wilderness

I find a small hotel close by, shower and doctor my wound. Supper. I am directed around the corner to a restaurant. A group of rather drunk young men call me over. A beer is offered. I ask for food and a woman wearing a T-shirt with the logo "Don't ignore the small things - a kite flies because of its tail" takes a bowl, ladles soup into it, chops off some pieces of a cooked duck that lies on the table, drops them into the bowl and brings it to me. One-pot restaurant. Takes the hassle of trying to make a menu selection in Vietnamese...

Now it is head down and knock off the miles north.

I deviate slightly to ride along the famed China Beach, one of the main R&R areas for US soldiers during the war. It is a disappointment - as sad and desolate as an unpopulated beach on a rainy, overcast day can be. The sea is ugly and threatening with a wicked side wash, Da Nang disappearing into mist and rain squalls in the distance.

Nearing the city I come across the Marble Mountains - a "popular pilgrimage site" the guidebook tells me. But long before I reach these iconic mountains rising out of the plain, I am ambushed by motorcycle touts who pull up alongside me as I ride, calling, "Hey, you go Da Nang? You want...?"

I try to ignore them but they are persistent. I want to say, Look, whether I'm going to Da Nang or not is my business, not yours... but what's the point?

I have no doubt that the Marble Mountains are well worth visiting, rich in history, religious significance and beauty. But for me, I'd rather just ride on. The streets around the mountains are cluttered with hundreds of shops all selling exactly the same bad copies of marble statues, all with their owners out on the pavement calling and waving, "Hey, motorcycle! You come -"

No thanks. It's ruined for me. I'd rather not see it.

And I didn't.

For most of the morning, rain had been threatening but as I enter Da Nang it begins to hammer down, the wind blowing at knock-your-bike-down gale force directly from the front. Already I can feel those disturbing wet patches getting through into my underclothes. I can see it's going to be one of those grit-your-teeth-and-endure days that all motorcycle travellers encounter at some point in their lives. It can't be helped but it would be better if I had a decent set of wet-weather gear.

After Da Nang, the road claws its way up a dramatic pass over a ridge that rises to over 500m and drops vertically into the sea. With the wind and rain and a heavy mist covering the highest point and reducing visibility to only a few metres, it makes for exciting riding.

Down the other side and out of the mist, but the rain persists. I pass Hue, the town that saw the bloodiest battles of the 1968 Tet offensive. Hue was occupied with little resistance by North Vietnamese and Viet Cong troops; shortly afterwards the Communists arrived and what followed was an indication of what would result from a North Vietnamese victory over the South: Communist cadres started to round up all those believed to be enemies of the people, bourgeoisie elements that needed to be eliminated if the purity of the Communist revolution was to be achieved. Hue was only under Communist control for twenty five days but during that period about three thousand civilians - land owners, merchants, Buddhist monks, Catholic priests, intellectuals, South Vietnamese government officials - were shot, buried alive, clubbed to death and buried in shallow graves. (Let's be honest and balanced here: the atrocities committed by ideologically driven North Vietnamese soldiers, military and political leaders were as egregious as those committed by the Americans.)

It took ten days for combined US and South Vietnamese troops to drive the North Vietnamese and VC out but not after the centre of Hue was destroyed and over 10,000 people, mostly civilians, had been killed.

Then on, past Hue, heading inland, away from the sea, the driving rain and numerous trucks on the road making riding increasingly dangerous.

By four I am cold, wet, miserable and badly in need of a hot shower. I find somewhere to stay in the town of Dong Ha but discover too late that there is a karaoke bar just outside my window...

Tomorrow I leave the coast and head inland towards Hanoi.

A blessed day.

I awake and look out of my window and it is no longer raining. Heavily overcast and cold, but no rain.

I pack up, load the bike and head out of town looking for the turnoff away from the congested coast road into the interior. My GPS tells me to turn left but I see no road. Then, at the last minute, a small track appears, blocked almost immediately by a herd of sleek-skinned cattle. This is the kind of road I like. I ride on, almost alone, more cows, chickens, sleepy dogs and water buffalo than vehicles; villages half hidden in the underbrush flash by with small patches of vegetables cut out of forest clearings, banana trees and ponds for ducks. I pause on a rickety metal bridge over a clear river and switch off the engine.

Clear in the silence of the bush I hear a cock crow. There must be a village or settlement nearby. And I find myself saying aloud, "Oh, this is beautiful -" Not tourist beautiful; few would want to travel here to look long at this scene; but, for me, its beauty lies in its isolation, its purity, the verdant abundance of its growth, its unspoilt naturalness.

With my helmet off, I sit on the bike a long while, allowing my ears to become attuned to the faint sounds of the bush around me, seeing the clear water tug at weeds growing long and bright green under the bridge arches below me.

Then, reluctantly, I start the engine and ride on slowly through rubber plantations, the edges of the road thick with flowering lantana, their yellow, orange and pink flowers and cloying perfume reminding me of my youth, walking through whispering sugar cane fields on the Natal coast, north of Durban, the cane breaks thick with flowering lantana.

I take a side road off another side road and find myself riding along the banks of a wide, slow-flowing river; children stand in small sampans and hook weed from the river bottom with long curved poles. Their laughter and chatter comes to me clear in the still air.

In the distance, the blue humps of karst mountains loom closer and then I am amongst them, their steep, heavily-wooded sides covered with a pernicious vine which threatens to smother everything, carpeting bamboo, palms, 40-ft trees, underbrush, telephone poles with a web of green tendrils and creating a subterranean world of darkness underneath, impossible to penetrate. Japanese knotweed, I find out later. It is no wonder this Triffid-like menace that can take over entire mountains attracts legal sanctions in the UK if allowed to spread onto a neighbour's land.

I discover that I have entered the Phong Nha-Ke Bang Nature Reserve, remote, heavily wooded and mountainous, and press on north. In a small field a man plods behind a single-share plough pulled by one ox; women congregate around a trailer parked on a river bank, laughing as they scoop live fish, just caught, into plastic buckets.

All day I ride through this wilderness, willing it not to end. My GPS tells me this too is part of the HCMT and I'm pleased to be on it again. It makes me feel, just tenuously I know, in touch with the men who cut these trails through the forest so many years ago.

* * * * *

I mean we were crazy, but it's built into the culture. It's like institutionalised insanity. When you're in combat, you can do basically what you want as long as you don't get caught. You can get away with murder. And the beautiful thing about the military is there's always somebody that can serve up as a scapegoat. Like Calley. I wonder why they didn't get Delta Company 1-9 because of Cam Ne. We were real scared. But President Johnson came out and defended us. But like that was before My Lai. When they did My Lai, I got nervous again. I said My God, and they have us on film.

From "Bloods" by Wallace Terry

Hanoi and the backpacker bike shuttle

And so, I come to my last day on the bike. It's cold and heavily overcast but, thank the Lord, not raining. I make good progress on the 420km leg to Hanoi, the land mostly wild and sparsely populated, the road virtually clear of traffic. Slowly, however, signs of human habitation appear: fields of rice, growing well now since I first passed this way; then maize and sugar cane, the sellers of cut cane increasing in number on the sides of the road. Villages become more numerous, then towns, the air hazing with pollution and the foul smoke of burning refuse.

Around midday I come unexpectedly upon another area of karst mountains, so distinctive to this part of the world, the dark rock rising almost vertically out of the lush green rice paddies. It takes over an hour to get through them but, sadly, the air pollution and smoke is so bad that within a few hundred metres they begin to blur into outline and fade away.

Then, suddenly, with just 50ks to go, I am ensnared once again into the cacophony of downtown traffic, a horror-story of congestion and chaos and noise. I nudge and shoulder my way into the city centre and check my GPS for accommodation, look down the list for hostels and, on the second go, I find backpackers' heaven, the half-brother of the other place in HCMC. It is equally congested, the pavements lined with that sorry breed of small bikes that are sold to and by backpackers who pick them up in Hanoi for $200 or so, ride them to HCMC, sell them again for $200 to other equally unsuspecting young people who ride them back to Hanoi - and so it goes on, a shuttle service for badly worn bikes. I'm quite sure most of them are never serviced, just repaired at some roadside joint with a hammer, screw driver and monkey wrench when they break down as, by the look of them, they must do fairly often.

I met an American guy whose bike's engine seized the day after he bought it. The up side is that repairs are cheap. A reconditioned engine cost him all of two million Dong - which sounds a lot but is, in fact, only $100. Two young Dutch backpackers whom I met last night also had bought bikes. The guy's chain had broken on the first day and his gear lever fell off on the second. They had no idea at all about bikes so I offered to look them over. The one bike was OK; the other, ridden by a young lass, was a suicide machine. The chain was almost dragging along the ground, the rear tyre worn bald to the canvas; I pulled the gear lever off with my fingers - stripped pinch bolt; oil dripped steadily from under the engine and the rear wheel bearings were shot.

I did what I could and suggested that they stop at the first roadside workshop they came to and, at the very least, replace the rear tyre, wheel bearings and gear lever.

But they will ride the bikes to HCMC and sell them on to another pair of excited but clueless youngsters and they, in turn, will ride them back to Hanoi. It's not a big deal. Breaking down is part of the experience. It's not an adventure until something goes wrong, so they say. Repairs are easy and cheap. Not many get injured badly. It's part of growing up and I love to see them, bright-eyed and filled with wanderlust, that enthusiasm that comes with youth and all the possibilities of exploring the world.

A redeeming feature of Hanoi, something that allows one briefly to excuse the notorious traffic (they sell T-shirts with pictures of the scooter-clogged streets, making a virtue of necessity) are the trees: large figs, their aerial roots hanging down over roads and pavements as if seeking water. They give the city a coolness, an exotic quality that is pleasing. It still has the traffic, the rats-nests of wires hanging from every pole and building, the street vendors and ad hoc pavement cafes where entrepreneurial women set up pots on street corners, arrange their blue and red children's plastic chairs along the wall on the pavement and begin selling food. I must admit I wasn't brave enough to try some. Seeing the yellow clawing legs of a whole duck rising and falling from a witch's brew of bubbles and steam in a large pot doesn't awaken my taste buds. Nor does watching women, crouched on their hams on the pavement, chopping up with cleavers bits of pig flesh, still living fish whose wide mouths continue to gasp for air even when half their body is already in the pot, waxy-legged, de-feathered ducks with staring dead eyes lying on pieces of wood amid the flies and the rubbish.

Street food - not for the faint-hearted.

To cater for the tourist trade, the town centre is crammed with shops selling the usual rubbish, things that are bought and taken home to sit incongruous on a shelf, gathering dust, until thrown away. Shops selling original rip-off paintings, any style you want, wait and watch while they paint your personal Gauguin, Cezanne or Matisse; displays of pictures painted with thread, embroidery so fine it takes the breath away, water-colours of silk. The large, tree-lined lake in the middle of the city provides a focus, a meeting place under the shade on benches set in gardens whose litter-free bright colours speak of a pride in this city so often missing in the public spaces of other cities. Couples meet and relax on benches in the shade of dark-leaved fig trees, old men attempt to hook fish with hand lines, throwing bread onto the surface of the water as bait. Two young girls in their late teens sit next to me as I rest alongside the lake and engage me in conversation, practicing their English, insisting on taking my email address and the obligatory selfie.

And, of course, there are the motorcycle repair shops to cater for the locals and the tourists whose dilapidated wrecks, easily identified by the rough, welded metal frames extending over the back wheel for strapping down a rucksack, which always need something repaired. These repair shops are usually no more than 5ft wide, open onto the pavement, with bits of engine, old tyres, scavenged leftovers from previous repairs filling the cubicle and forcing the mechanic to work on the pavement between the feet of passing pedestrians, tools and parts and dismembered bikes surrounding him as he peers at an engine, a pony-tailed, sandaled backpacker peering worriedly over his shoulder.

I have a few days before I fly home. Halong Bay on the coast beckons. It is the jewel of Vietnam, World Heritage Site, with one thousand nine hundred and sixty nine islands, must-see for all tourists, so they say.

I wonder who counted the islands?

* * * * *

We came back totally fucked up in the head. But it took ten years for our bodies to catch up to where our heads were. All of a sudden you feel this psychological pain become physical pain. Then if you're lucky, which I was, somebody come up and pull your coat and say, "Hey, you need some help." 'Cause if my old lady hadn't decided I needed some help, I would probably either be dead or in jail today.

This psychological thing, we try to suppress it. But it kills us quicker than if somebody just walked up to you and put a bullet in your head. 'Cause it eats away at your inner being. It eats away at everything that you ever learned in life. Your integrity. Your word. See, that's all you have.

Vietnam taught you to be liar. To be a thief. To be dishonest. To go against everything you ever learned. It taught you everything you did not need to know, because you were livin' a lie. And the lie was you ain't have no business bein' there in the first place. You wasn't here for democracy. You wasn't protecting your homeland. And that was what wear you down. We were programmed for the fact as American fighting men that we were still fighting a civilized war. And you don't fight a civilized war. It's nothing civilized about - about war.

From "Bloods" by Wallace Terry

Halong Bay and a girls' night out

I am reluctant. The biscuit-tin scenes of Halong Bay that grace every tourist office wall somehow do not attract me. Nor does the fact that, so I read in the brochure, 4000 tourist boats a day ply these waters. An aquatic equivalent of the roads.

But I have the time, I am here, so I decide to go. Once again, it's easier to take an organised tour. Cheaper, less hassle. And I won't have to ride through a hundred kilometres of stinking, demented traffic to get there and back.

And it's not so easy to die on these roads travelling by bus.

Somehow our junk, the Golden Bay, doesn't look anything like the pictures in the brochure. It seems to have aged somewhat in the intervening years. Calling it a *junk* is perhaps appropriate. However, it floats and the beds are comfortable, even though I am concerned that I will fall through the rotten deck planking and there are holes in the hull you could stick your fist through. Fortunately the sea is habitually calm in Halong Bay. A hand-operated windlass is fitted to the stern deck to lift a hand-made anchor. It has a certain charm that only decrepitude can bring. The atmosphere just wouldn't have been the same on a sleek, fibreglass boat.

I know, I have breached the adventure bikers' code once again and signed on for a two-day, all-inclusive tour of the bay. So shoot me.

The tour is crummy but slick; our group multicultural and friendly - Auzzies, of course - you can't go anywhere in the world without meeting a few of them; Germans, Danes, South American, a handful of Brits, South Korean. All communicate in the universal language of travellers, English, and a convivial time is had by all.

We are promised a "welcome drink" and I look forward to a tall glass of something faintly alcoholic, beaded with condensation, a little paper umbrella... but it turns out to be a cup of sweet, black tea.

The bus trip there lasts nearly four hours. Then a bicycle trip to a cave. We are dropped off on an island by motor launch to collect our bikes - death traps used and abused by a thousand tourists siphoned along the same conduit to the same crummy cave and back; rusting chains, flat tyres, defective brakes. Two chains come off on the way but we manage to get them on again. At the path leading to the cave, we wait while a tourist party in front of us files back to collect their equally dodgy bicycles. Then into the cave.

It was... well, a cave.

Back on the good ship Golden Bay, the hot water is cold but the drinks are free between 6 and 7, which is a boon. Later, after a few beers, a young German lad wonders why the world still likes them despite... well, you know.

I have been allocated a room with two young lasses: Lucky (well, I'm lucky, granted, but her name is "Lucky") from South Korea and Isobel from Germany. They share the double bed and treat me like one of the girls. After supper, Lucky produces Korean face packs and the three of us lie on our beds with wet, rice-paper facemasks softening our skin followed by mutual back and shoulder massages. Lots of giggling from the girls (I don't do giggling much) and selfies and banter - a 21-year-old German, a 38-year-old South Korean and a 64-year-old geezer sharing a room. I suppose, in essence, that's part of what travel is all about.

And I always wondered what young ladies did on a girls' night out...

On the bus trip back, we are stopped by some cops. "Paying the government," our tour guide informs us wryly. I ask him to explain. He tells me that tour buses are regularly targeted by the police. The driver either pays the "fine" - usually about $20 - or goes through the legalities of filling in forms at the police station, an administrative nightmare that takes hours so it's easier just to pay the bribe.

On the bus I sit next to a retired Canadian banker who is advising the Vietnamese government on how to reduce corruption and nepotism which, he tells me, is endemic.

Across the isle two Brazilian lads use their mobile phones to make contact with young prostitutes in Hanoi. I watch as they flick through images of sweet-faced Vietnamese girls, selecting as one would pick goods off a supermarket shelf. To each young lass the same message: "Hello, how are you? I'll soon be in Hanoi..."

The girls - I suppose one would call them prostitutes but they seem too young, their expressions too innocent for that; maybe students looking for a creative way of supplementing their incomes during their studies. Maybe their on-line faces are like the photographs of the *Golden Bay* seen in the brochures - nothing at all like the reality. I don't know. It's a part of life that mercifully has passed me by, somehow distasteful. Perhaps I'm just old, from a different generation, but I don't think so.

I hope not.

Back at the hostel I find a tall, loose-boned man sitting on a bed across from me. He sees my helmet and says, "You a biker?" It's not really a question.

I nod, lifting my helmet in acknowledgement.

His name is Tom, a Canadian. He's on his way into China for a six-month trip. Found a way round the Chinese restriction on foreign travellers riding their own bikes through the country without the inhibiting and expensive presence of a "guide". He tells me he will enter China as a foot-passenger and then buy a second-hand Chinese bike, tour the country for six months and then sell it again. He's sure it can be done.

When he stands I notice that there is an awkwardness in his movements. "You seem to be favouring your left hand," I say to him in my blunt South African way. "You had an accident?"

He uses his left hand to raise his right that he has loosely tucked into a pocket. The arm is thin and stick-like, the hand limp and dead. He waggles the arm a few times then tucks the hand back into the pocket that holds it in place.

"My right arm's useless," he tells me. "About ten years ago I came off my bike and hit a tree. It ripped all the muscles and nerves out of my shoulder."

"So how do you ride then?" I ask him.

"With one arm," he tells me.

*****

Now I was looking beyond the physical appearance of the Vietn'ese and lookin' at the people themselves. They were very pleasant, very outgoing, very beautiful people. I started disliking myself for what America, the war, and bein' in the Army had caused me to become.

But I was still a animal.

From "Bloods" by Wallace Terry

Conclusion - I finally learned how to live...

By the time I got home, the wound in my foot had become infected. I went to A&E and they operated on me within twelve hours - opened up the wound, cleaned it out, pinned all the broken bones together.

I limped about for three months. My little toe is still shorter than it ought to be and it sticks out sideways a bit. Annoying because it always catches on my sock.

Small price to pay for the opportunity to enter into the lives, for a brief time, of a kind and gracious people...

* * * * *

But my moms, she brought me back 'cause she loved me. And I think because I loved her. She kept reminding me what type of person I was before I left. Of the dreams I had promised her before I left. To help her buy a home and make sure that we was secure in life.

And she made me see the faces again. See Vietnam. See the incidents. She made me really get ashamed of myself for doin' the things I had done. You think no crime is a crime durin' war, 'specially when you get way with it. And when she made me look back at it, it just didn't seem it was possible for me to be able to do those things to other people, because I value life. That's what moms and grandmoms taught me as a child.

From "Bloods" by Wallace Terry

* * * * *

Excerpt from "When Heaven and Earth Changed Places" - Le Ly Hayslip. (Le Ly had a child by an American soldier who later deserted her. Eventually, after the war, she managed to emigrate with her child to America and begin a new life.)

Once my father was properly buried, and his soul dwelled comfortably in our spirit house, I discovered that a good many things had been buried with him. I was no longer confused about where my duty lay - with the Viet Cong? With the legal government and its allies? With the peasants in the countryside?

No - my duty lay with my son, and with nurturing life, period. My father taught me this on our hilltop years before, as the night of war was falling, but only now was this duty as clear as the morning sun. I no longer had to struggle with myself to achieve it day by day. I only had to love and love and act in concert with those feelings.

My father himself had demonstrated this principle many times in his life, most recently when he forgave me for my sin of chua hoam - *becoming an unwed mother - and embraced my little child to his heart. He had not been angry at me for bringing new life into the world - far from it! He was angry that I did it in such a way that my child was denied a father. After all, where would I myself be - how long would I have survived a war that claimed so many others - without my father to guide me? Through him, I learned that although great love alone cannot remove all obstacles, it certainly puts no new ones in the path toward peace: between soldiers, civilians, and between a woman and herself.*

I saw that a determination to live, no matter what, was more powerful than a willingness to die. Just as the Christians believed Jesus gave his life so that they might live forever, I believed my father's death was his way of giving me eternal peace - not in the hereafter, but for every instant of every day I was alive.

Vietnam already had too many people who were ready to die for their beliefs. What it needed was men and women - brothers and sisters - who refused to accept either death or death-dealing as a solution to their problems. If you keep compassion in your heart, I discovered, you never long for death yourself. Death and suffering, not people, become your enemy; and anything that lives is your ally. It was as if, by realising this, an enormous burden had been lifted from my young shoulders. From my father's death, I had finally learned how to live.

Other books by Lawrence Bransby

Travelogues:

There are no Fat People in Morocco
Venture into Russia - Three Motorcycle Journeys
The Wakhan Corridor - A Motorcycle Journey into Central Asia
By Motorcycle through Vietnam - Reflections on a Gracious People
A Pass too Far - Travels in Central Asia The Plymouth-Dakar Old Bangers Rally
A Walk to Lourenco Marques - Reminiscences of a 12-year-old
By Bicycle to Beira - Reminiscences of a 14-year-old

Adult Novels:

A Matter of Conscience
Life-Blood - Earth-Blood
Second-Sailor, Other Son

Young Adult Novels:

Down Street
Homeward Bound
A Geek in Shining Armour
A Mountaintop Experience
Of Roosters, Dogs and Cardboard Boxes
The Boy who Counted to a Million
Outside the Walls
Remember the Whales